Rainbow Lorikeet

Rainbow Lorikeets as pets

Rainbow Lorikeet Keeping, Pros and Cons, Care, Housing, Diet and Health.

By

Roger Rodendale

ALL RIGHTS RESERVED. This book contains material protected under International and Federal Copyright Laws and Treaties.

Any unauthorized reprint or use of this material is strictly prohibited. No part of this book may be reproduced or transmitted in any form or by any means, electronic, mechanical or otherwise, including photocopying or recording, or by any information storage and retrieval system without express written permission from the author.

Copyright © 2017

Published by: Zoodoo Publishing

Table of Contents

Table of Contents 3

Introduction 4

Chapter 1: The Magnificent Rainbow Lorikeet 6

Chapter 2: Bringing The Lorikeet Home 14

Chapter 3: When You Bring the Lorikeet Home 32

Chapter 4: Rainbow Lorikeet Care Guide 43

Chapter 5: Bonding With The Rainbow Lorikeet 61

Chapter 6: Rainbow Lorikeet Breeding 78

Chapter 7: Rainbow Lorikeet Healthcare 86

Chapter 8: Cost of Having a Rainbow Lorikeet 110

Conclusion 111

References 112

Introduction

The rainbow lorikeet is one of the most unmistakable species of parrots. This parrot of Australian origin is the most colorful of all its cousins; the vibrant hues of blue, yellow, violet, green, red, orange and indigo earned this species its name.

While most people choose the bird as a pet for its overwhelming beauty, they soon realize that these birds also have an endearing personality to match. They are extremely playful birds. They love spending time with their owners, indulging in a good deal of play and interaction.

These birds are extremely intelligent, which means that they need more than just food and shelter to be healthy. They need constant mental stimulation and a lot of attention from their owners.

Food and care is also quite specific with these birds. After all, they are an exotic species. Good care is essential to also ensure that these birds do not suffer from any health issues. If you are new to the world of parrots, you will need ample information about these birds before you decide to open your home to them.

This book gives you all the information that you will need about the birds. It talks in detail about the natural habitat, dietary preferences, behavior, breeding and lots more. That way, you can give the bird exactly what it needs to be healthy.

Being a responsible owner means that you need to be equipped with as much information as possible. That way, in case you meet any unexpected hurdles, you will be able to help the bird and yourself overcome them.

With parrots, the fact that they are highly intelligent makes them more of a challenge than other birds. They analyze everything. That is why you need to be very careful from the time the bird enters your home until he is settled. (Please note: although there are female birds of this species, we will refer to them as 'he' for ease). Providing a stress free environment is the first step towards building a good relationship with your bird.

This book provides you with step-by-step instructions that will help you with everything throughout your journey with your lorikeet. Remember that these birds are going to be with you for 20 years or more. So, learn as much as you can about the bird before you bring one home. This book is the perfect start for you.

Chapter 1: The Magnificent Rainbow Lorikeet

The rainbow lorikeet is one of the most beautifully colored birds in the parrot family. These birds belong to a group that is classified as true parrots.

1. What are true parrots?

There are about 350 species of parrots that are classified as true parrots. Most of these birds are magnificently colored. These birds are found world over including in areas in Mexico, South and Central America, India, Sub-Saharan regions of Africa, South East Asia, Australia and even in Polynesia.

These birds have a few characteristics that are common to all species:

- They have a curved beak. The jaw can move slightly over the area where the beak connects with the skull.

- They usually have an upright posture.

- These birds are known to be among the most intelligent of all bird groups. They have a very high cranial capacity, which often makes them good at talking and mimicking.

- These birds have very good flying abilities.

- They also have great climbing skills.

- The ability to mimic sounds comes from the fact that they have a certain vocal organ called the syrinx that is present just below the trachea.

- These birds are omnivorous. Their diet mostly consists of seeds, nuts and fruits, but they may also indulge in insects and small prey animals sometimes.

- These birds usually make nests in tree cavities. They are monogamous, which means that they choose one partner for life.

True parrots make up the super family Psittacoidea and two primary sub families, namely *Psittacinae and Loriinae.* These sub families have been categorized into several other families and sub species.

2. Physical description of rainbow lorikeets

The name given to these birds is very apt. They have a violet colored head with an orange red upper breast. The abdomen has a blue margin with some traces of red. The back of these birds is bright green in color.

The tail is greenish-yellow in color. The beak is a beautiful reddish orange color that ends in a yellow tip. The belly of the bird has deep green feathers. The rump and the thighs are yellow in color with margins of deep green feathers. When the bird is in flight, you can see the contrasting yellow wing bar and the bright red coverts in the under wing.

In the case of the juveniles, the beak is usually black in color. Their coloration is not as bright. The bill is shorter and so is the body and wings.

You cannot tell the difference between the male and the female adults. This is called dimorphism, where the male and female look identical.

Of course, upon close observation, you will notice a few differences. They also have some behavioral differences that are quite noticeable. These tips will help you distinguish between a male and female rainbow lorikeet:

- The female has a slightly smaller head than the male. They are smaller in size overall.

- The size of the beak is smaller in the case of the female rainbow lorikeet.

- Male rainbow lorys will have a larger number of dark orange feathers on the breast. The females on the other hand have a more yellowish tinge to the breast feathers. It looks almost like the yellow color bleeds into the orange color of the breast feathers.

- The male looks more robust in the chest area. His head also seems squarer. In the case of females, the head is rounded.

- You will see a distinct difference in behavior during the mating season. The male will usually puff his chest up and hop around his partner while she feeds. This is to make sure that there is no competitor for her food. This also keeps other birds from interrupting here whilst she eats.

Rainbow lorikeet stats:
- Size: Medium
- Body length (head to tail): 30 cms.
- Wing Size: 15 cms
- Weight: 133 g

3. Habitat and range

Rainbow lorikeets are found in a variety of different natural habitats. They inhabit open forests, woodland, rainforests, mangroves, water edges, gardens and parks. While they are mostly considered to be lowland species, they can also be found in the mountainous regions of Australia. These birds are considered to be altitudinal migrants.

When commonly lowland species move to higher altitudes for a short span in a particular season, they are called altitudinal migrants. The Rainbow lorikeets return to the lowlands during the breeding season.

They have a rather wide geographical distribution. Here are some areas that these birds are usually found in:

- Northern Australia: The region between Kimberley and Cape York.

- East Australia: They are seen east coast most often.

- South Australia: They are normally found in the Eyre Peninsula.

- Other regions: Besides Australia, they are also found in Indonesia, Solomon Islands, Papua New Guinea, New Caledonia and Vanuatu.

- There are several factors that determine the movement of these birds, including the reproductive cycle and the availability of food.

- A lot of local population has migrated to areas where food sources have been introduced in the suburban gardens.

- These birds are nomadic and will migrate in search of food.

4. Diet and feeding habits

In the wild, the main source of protein for these birds is pollen. This is also one of the largest components of their diet. Lorikeets are known for consuming nectar. They normally target blossoms from plants and trees like Proteacea, Myrtaceae and Xanthoroaceae.

In addition to this, they also consume berries, seeds and fruits. They may occasionally eat insects like thrips, ants, beetles, wasps and weevils. They will also consume larvae like moth larvae, fly maggots and weevil larvae.

Since they are attracted to fruits like mangos, pears and apples, these birds can cause severe damage to orchards. They also tend to feed on crops of sorghum and maize. They feed on the grains that are unripe.

Rainbow lorikeets exhibit the following behavior when it comes to feeding:

- They eat all day long.

- They spend 70% of their day feeding.

- In the morning, a feeding session can last for up to 4 hours.

- In order to fulfill their daily requirements, they have to feed for at least 2-5 hours.

- They have a high rate of feeding. For instance, they can consume up to 40 Eucalyptus flowers in one minute.

- During these bouts of feeding, they take small breaks of about 10 seconds to look around and make sure that they are not under any threat by a predator.

- They target the flowers that have blossomed on the outer foliage of trees.

- During the warmer months of the year, they take a break from feeding in the middle of the day. Then they return to the feeding area when it gets cooler.

- Rainbow lorikeets travel up to 50 kms each day in the search of food.

- They consume water that is trapped in the leaves. Sometimes, they may drink surface water from ponds or lakes.

- They have a peculiar arrangement of toes and the beak, which allows them to perform entertaining acrobatics while feeding.

5. Rainbow lorikeet in folk tales

Rainbow lorikeets have been in close association with human beings for centuries now. It is no wonder that these native birds have become part of several folk tales.

One of the most popular ones is about how the rainbow lorikeet got its beautiful colors.

The lorikeet was a plain white bird. However, all the birds in the Australian outback had beautiful colors. The lorikeet had short wings and a tail and he had small black eyes. This made the lorikeet very sad.

So, he decided to ask the birds for ideas to get colors like them. None of them knew how they had developed these beautiful colors, so they thought hard about how to help the lorikeet.

The first idea that they came up with was to fly through the waterfall as the sun shone on it. They headed out to the great waterfall and the lorikeet zipped through the water. However, he still stayed white.

Then, they went to a meadow with the most colorful flowers. There were all kinds of flowers there: red, blue, orange, purple and more. The lorikeet was excited and flew through these flowers like a rocket. Still, he hadn't become colorful.

This made him very sad and he decided to stay alone for a while. Then, the Black Kyte who was looking for his dinner spotted the lonely and small lorikeet. He flew closer to him and the lorikeet fled for his life. He flew as fast as his wings could take him. He weaved and ducked to save himself.

Then, without even noticing, he flew straight through the middle of a bright and beautiful rainbow. When he came out, he had picked up the magnificent colors of the rainbow. The Kyte, blinded by these beautiful colors, flew straight into a gum tree. This gave the lorikeet enough time to fly home.

While this is a popular story, there is another story about Meeyla the Rainbow Lorikeet. She was a disabled girl who was bullied and teased by everyone. Her father sought out to the Great Spirit to help his daughter. They turned her into a beautiful rainbow lorikeet.

This is why even today, the rainbow lorikeet is very symbolic. If you encounter a rainbow lorikeet, it is a sign that you can overcome any issue just like Meeyla did her disability. The rainbow lorikeet's acrobatics and his way of hanging upside down is a symbol of taking a different perspective of things. That way, you will be able to find some new and exciting solutions to any problems.

While these are just folklores, the fact that the rainbow lorikeet is an essential part of Australian history cannot be stressed more.

6. Rainbow lorikeet negative impact

Rainbow lorikeets are definitely the most loved pets. However, when it comes to being in the wild, these birds are considered potential pests. They are also seen as a threat to the population of local species in places like New Zealand.

In fact, it is illegal to release captive rainbow lories into the wild in places like Auckland. This was following a possible release of captive birds deliberately in Auckland around the 1990s. These birds flourished and established a feral population of about 200 birds. There are several reasons why these birds are seen as an unwanted organism as per the Biosecurity Act that was passed in the region in the year 1993.

A threat to local bird species

There is a lot of evidence to suggest that these birds tend to dominate any food source in an area. They have the ability to dislodge several species of birds, even some that are much larger than them.

These birds are also carriers of several avian diseases that can spread to local species, causing a decline in their numbers.

One of the most popular instances of a species being excluded by rainbow lories is that of the Tui bird in New Zealand. Both these species depend on nectar feeders. Most species of birds try to defend their food sources in pairs or as per the pecking order.

In the case of rainbow lories, an entire flock defends a particular food source. That way, they are able to displace an entire species. Therefore, several birds that feed on honey and nectar will face competition from rainbow lorikeets.

They are also heavy competition for birds that nest in cavities. Rainbow lorikeets compete for the roosting sites and nesting sites of these birds.

In addition to all of this, these birds also damage several crops and orchards. They impact orchards of apples and grapes, along with other soft fruit. They are also a threat in areas that have vineyards. They tend to harm the commercial fruit industry quite significantly when feral populations are high.

These negative impacts of the bird have led to several feral populations being eradicated from different parts of the world. The goal is to make sure that they are not allowed to establish in the wild.

When these birds can be identified, they are sent back to the owners. In some cases, they are sent to secure captive facilities.

These birds are proliferous breeders. They can produce 3-4 clutches in one breeding season. That is why it is very important for rainbow lorikeet owners to keep them in cages that are very secure.

You can also get in touch with respective authorities in your country if you notice large populations of these birds in the wild. While it is legal to breed these birds in captivity and keep them as pets, you can face heavy fines if your bird escapes into the wild.

Chapter 2: Bringing The Lorikeet Home

When you decide to bring home your rainbow lorikeet, there are several sources that you can look at. You have the option of independent breeders, pet stores, rescue shelters and of course, simply fostering.

But before you find a source for your lorikeet, the question that you need to ask yourself is whether you are really ready for a lorikeet or not.

Brining a bird home is not as simple as putting him in a cage and leaving some food in a bowl. Rainbow lorikeets require a good deal of attention from your end. These highly intelligent birds require a lot of mental stimulation. You need to make sure that you keep the birds in good health. Of course, there are a lot of things like accidents on your favorite couch or your favorite artifact being chewed up that you need to be prepared for before your bird is fully trained.

In this chapter, we will look at the pros and cons of having rainbow lorikeets as pets. Once you are sure about bringing one home, you can look for the different sources to buy your bird from.

1. Do rainbow lorikeets make good pets?
Rainbow lorikeets are among the most popular pets. They are known for their beautiful plumage. In addition to that, these birds have an infectious personality that makes them great house pets.

That said, rainbow lorikeets are best for those who are committed to their pets. They should be interested in spending time with their pets and with providing quality care to their birds. If you do not have enough time to spend with your pet, then the rainbow lorikeet is not the bird for you.

These birds are extremely affectionate and quite funny, too. They bond with their owners strongly. That is why you need to be prepared for 20 odd years of giving your bird ample time every day.

Just like any other parrot, the rainbow lorikeet also needs a lot of play. These birds love to chew, so stocking up on toys that they can destroy is a good idea. These toys are available in pet stores and online. They are made of safe material such as soft wood. This is a great way for the bird to exercise.

Another thing about lorikeets is that they are exceptionally messy birds. Most often, pet birds are difficult to clean up after as they are messy. But, a lorikeet has a diet that is mostly liquid based. This makes them poop around the clock.

You need to house the bird in an area where you do not have too many carpets and around floors and walls that are easy to clean. You can even consider using a plastic lining on the floor or the wall to protect it. Of course, these birds are so intelligent that they can be potty trained. It takes some effort, but we will discuss this in the following chapters.

If you are able to take care of the special needs of this bird, you may consider bringing a rainbow lorikeet home. However, you need to get as much information as you can before you actually decide to bring one into your home.

You can look for multiple sources to bring your lorikeet home from. In the following section, we will discuss the most feasible options.

2. Finding a good breeder

It is easy to find a list of local breeders in your area. The hard part is making sure that they are 'good' breeders. You can begin by looking at classified ads for birds for sale. If you find any listing promising, you can contact the breeder.

Today, you have the option of looking online as well. There are various breeder directories that will list the best breeders in your city or even in your locality.

With the Internet providing free advertising, there are several breeders who are listed when you look for one in your vicinity. You will probably find several websites that will show up with the name and location. It is best that you visit the aviary before you fall for cheap discounts or sales online.

Here are a few tips that will help you find a good breeder to buy your pet from:

- The breeder should have clean aviaries that are not rusty and shabby.

- The food and water bowls should not have any bird feces in them.

- The birds must not have ruffled feathers or any deformities.

- Proper quarantining measures should be taken for any bird that is sick or suspected of carrying any illness.

- When you approach a bird, he should be curious. If he sticks to a corner on the floor of the cage, he is probably unwell.

- The breeder should be willing to answer all your queries with respect to the lorikeet.

- A closed aviary system where birds from other flocks are restricted is a good option. The aviaries also insist that you wash your hands thoroughly or change your boots before you enter the premises where the birds are kept. This is the best option, as the risk of illness is very low.

You can look for recommendations from previous clients of the breeder if possible. A good breeder will also help you meet the birds that have been bought from him. You can also sign up for email lists and groups. You can join these groups on popular online groups such as Yahoo groups. Through these groups, you can read testimonials, get newsletters and also online magazines that will help you find the perfect breeder to source a healthy rainbow lorikeet from.

3. Questions to ask your breeder

After you have located a good breeder in your area, you will have to make sure that you meet them or visit the facility. There are a few things that are advantageous for bird owners to make sure that their birds are a perfect fit for their home. Here are a few questions that you should ask before buying from a breeder:

Are the birds hand-raised?
Not too long ago, finding birds that were hand-raised were easy to find. You could probably find them with breeders, but not really in pet stores. Today, the picture is quite different, with hand-raised birds being the preferred choice. Even in pet stores, they are hand-raised to make them tamer and more social when it comes to human beings.

Hand-raised birds are those that have been removed when they are hatchlings and then raised by human beings. Some breeders and pet stores will co-parent with the parent birds, but the babies are not raised entirely by the parents.

This makes the bird people oriented. That way, you have a "pet" from the time the bird enters your home. The bird will probably even step up on your finger or arm without much hesitation. These birds are less likely to bite as well. They do not perceive you or your hand as a threat.

When you visit a breeder, make sure that you ask for birds that are hand-tamed, unless you are willing to spend the time it requires to train the bird and make him tame. Breeders will not hand raise a bird most often because they do not have the time and the resources required. In most cases, these birds are shipped off to pet stores and are sold at much lower costs than one that is hand-tamed.

You will pay a price for this with a bird that may not become as tame as you want it to be. It is possible to make them social, but it requires careful training and probably a few nips from time to time.

When you pick a bird that you want to take home, it is a good idea to insist that you handle it. Even with birds that have been hand-raised, particularly with rainbow lorikeets that have a tendency to bluff, you will find them becoming nippy or skittish around people. This is a sign that the birds are not being hand-tamed.

With most places, the bird will be handled only until the time he doesn't need assistance to eat. Once the bird has been weaned, he will be left in the aviary with the other birds with very little human interaction. These birds are more oriented towards birds, in comparison to people. These birds will most often try to bite when you reach out for them.

Birds that have been weaned correctly and trained to be easy to handle will, no doubt, be more expensive. This is because of the effort involved in making them that way.

The younger you can buy your bird, the better it is. That way, you will not only have a hand fed-bird, but you can also make sure that he gets the attention that he needs after he has been weaned. Younger birds also adapt a lot faster than older ones.

Have the birds been weaned?
Most avian experts and experienced pet owners will discourage you from buying a bird that has not been weaned. The period of weaning can be really stressful on the babies and if you try to move them in that time, it gets even worse.

Research with popular veterinary facilities reveal that birds that have been sold or moved just before they are weaned are at a higher risk of developing health issues. This risk is greater if you already have pet birds at home and you have to introduce the new one to them. This is because the immune system is compromised with stress. It is true that birds that have already been weaned and are capable of feeding on their own are stronger in terms of immunity.

If you are new to the world of birds, hand feeding is not very easy. It is also risky. Even if you know of people who have been successful at doing so, it is best not to take a chance. It depends on the personality of the bird and each bird is different when it comes to hand feeding. Some are easier than others.

There is also room for a lot of error when you are new. For instance, the formula may be a little overheated. This can cause serious crop issues and irritation in the crop lining. As a result, the bird may develop many infections. This damage happens very fast between the time the baby has stopped eating and the food stops moving through the crop. You need some experience to recognize a possible problem.

If you have a breeder or a pet store trying really hard to sell you a baby bird that has not been weaned, they are possibly trying to save themselves from the trouble. This is passed on to you along with a lot of risk to the well being of the bird.

You will hear a lot of reasons like the bonding between you and your bird will be better or that he will love you more. In the wild, birds do not form permanent bonds unless they reach adulthood and have reached the breeding age. In the case of rainbow lorikeets, the fact that they are not monogamous also leaves you a lot of room to bond with your pet.

All you need to do is be willing to give the bird the time, train him, make sure that you feed him well and keep him healthy in order to form a strong bond. Lorikeets will form a strong bond with one owner in most cases but are a lot easier to adapt in comparison to any other parrot breed.

Does the bird only show a strong bond for one person?
If the breeder is able to bond with the bird and not anyone else from the family, say his wife, then there are chances that the bird will show a dislike for women in general. This behavior can be altered if you have the time for it. If not, you might want to look for a bird that is capable of bonding with others while maintaining one strong bond with one human. That is the safer option if you want to prevent accidents.

Is the bird prone to screaming or biting?
Very often, birds pick up bad behavior because people, unknowingly, reinforce them. For instance, giving the bird a treat to stop screaming or even giving him attention is a sign for the bird that it is acceptable to behave in that manner. While they pick these behavior patterns easily, it can be really hard to get rid of them.

You may notice that the bird is calm in the presence of new people but will soon show this behavior when he has adjusted to their presence. This is why it is best that you spend some time with your potential before buying one.

Remember, once you have brought the bird home, you need to even own any behavior quirks. They are certainly changeable. With some birds it may take a few days while with others it can take several months or even years. If that is the type of commitment you are willing to make, then consider a pet lorikeet. This can hamper your relationship with the bird if you are not willing to work on it.

How old is the bird?
This is a really important question for you to ask. With store bought birds, you may not be able to know the exact age, but an approximation at the very least is necessary. With older birds, training them is definitely more challenging. With birds that are too young, you will have to make additional efforts to keep them healthy while the immune system builds to its full capacity. A young, weaned bird is best when you are not very experienced with birds or if you do not have enough time.

4. What to look for when buying from a breeder

There are two things that you should be sure of when you buy from a breeder:
- The bird should be healthy
- The husbandry practices should be good.

Here are a few things to look for when you visit any aviary owned by a breeder:

The condition of the feathers
If you are handed a small, fluffy baby bird, it does seem cute and you may even believe that it is how they are supposed to look. However, by the time a baby rainbow lorikeet has been weaned, he is practically the size of an adult. The bird is able to perch like an adult and also has fully developed feathers.

If a bird has feathers that seem disheveled when they are younger, it is quite normal, as baby birds tend to be hard on their plumes. However, the down feathers should not stick out in between the colored feathers and through them. This is a sign that the bird is plucking his feathers or that the parents are doing so.

Bad plumage is also a sign that the bird has been weaned too early or has some disease. There are several serious illnesses in all species of parrots that will affect the feathers.

The activity level
If you notice that the bird is in a corner of the cage and continues to sleep even if you approach him, he is probably unwell. It is true that young birds sleep a lot more than adults. However, with anything that is interesting such as a new visitor, they will become alert. If you are unsure, visit the bird a couple of times more to see if the activity level improves.

Appearance of nostrils and eyes
In birds, infections ted to manifest in the form of an eye infection or a plugged nose or blocked sinus. If you notice that the eyes are cloudy or red or that the nostrils have some discharge, it is a definite sign of illness. If the infection is minor, it can be cured with simple medication. However, it is best that you wait for at least a week to check on the bird. You must ensure that this bird is quarantined even if he seems like he is perfect health when you buy him.

The weight of the bird
The bird that you are planning to buy should neither be overweight, nor should it be undernourished. The keel bone, which is present near the belly, just above the bird's legs is a good indicator of the body condition of the bird.

In adult birds, the bone should be in line with the flesh and must not protrude. In the case of baby birds, it tends to protrude a little after they have been weaned because they are usually active and also because they may lost some weight after weaning. If you notice that the bone is jutting out by more than $1/8^{th}$ of an inch, the bird still needs to develop before you take him home. In the case of an adult bird, that is a sign that the bird is malnourished and that he may also have underlying health issues.

Even when you are certain that your bird is healthy, make sure that you get a health guarantee. You see, in birds, it is hard to tell if they are healthy or not immediately. Should you notice any issues after the purchase, a health guarantee will be useful.

Health guarantee

With a reputable breeder, a health guarantee is provided with every specimen that they sell. If the seller has a health guarantee, it is an indication of good breeding practice.

With birds, it is always reasonable to believe that the bird may not be in the best of his health when you make a purchase. Should you have to return the bird, a health guarantee ensures that you get a full refund. It is best that you avoid breeders who do not provide a health guarantee.

Without a health guarantee, it is almost impossible for a buyer to prove that the breeder knew about the illness when he made a sale. With a written health guarantee, you can make up for this lack of legal protection on the part of the buyer.

A health guarantee works both ways. It protects a seller if the new owner is negligent. It also helps the buyer in case the breeder did not disclose any disease that the bird could be carrying. There are a few conditions that every health guarantee contains:

- The health of your bird is guaranteed for a total of three days as long as the bird has been thoroughly examined by a certified Avian Vet. This is an expense that you need to take care of.

  Should the veterinary clinic find any issues that makes the health of the bird unsatisfactory, you need a written documentation that will state the issues.

  You must return the bird immediately for a full refund. The species and the band number of the bird must be mentioned in the document provided. The breeder will not reimburse the vet fees or any expense that you have to bear for transportation.

- In case the bird dies within 12 days of purchase, you need to make sure that a necropsy is conducted within 72 hours after the death of the bird.

If you are not able to conduct the necropsy immediately, the body must be refrigerated until the tests are conducted.

The reports of the necropsy should be sent to the veterinarian of the breeder and must include the species and the band number. If these reports prove beyond any doubt that the bird had any health issues that originated before the purchase, you will be able to get a full refund or a replacement.

Some breeders will also allow you a 6-month window during which a death of the bird will ensure reimbursement provided a proper necropsy is conducted.

The breeder will not be held responsible for any expenses that you have to bear for these tests. You will also not hold the breeder liable if any bird from your existing flock develops any problem. It is mandatory to quarantine every new bird and if you do not do so, you cannot hold the breeder responsible.

- You must ensure that the bird has been quarantined adequately when you bring him home. He should be kept away from the other birds for at least 30 days before introducing him into the flock.

- If you already have other birds at home for a year or more, you will have to provide all the medical records of the bird and correct documentation for their health. It is possible that viruses that infect birds stay in a certain environment for many hours even after the bird has recovered fully.

- Negligence on the part of the owner does not make the breeder liable for any return or refund. For instance, if you leave the bird in the car on a hot day or if you do not provide the bird with adequate food and care, you cannot hold the breeder responsible for any health issues or even death.

Of course, a health guarantee does not cover for any behavioral or psychological issues. It is your responsibility to make sure that you spend time with the bird to understand his behavior before you make the purchase.

5. Choosing a pet store

This is the easiest option and therefore, most people choose to bring their birds home from a pet store. Most bird owners and bird lovers will advise you to refrain from this. The reason is that several pet stores buy from commercial breeders who rear the birds in miserable conditions. However, there are a few genuine pet stores who ensure good health of every bird that they keep.

You can find a great local pet store if you follow a few simple tips. However, before you do that, let us compare breeders and pets stores.

Buying from a breeder v/s buying from a pet store
For those who are looking for convenience, the pet store can seem like the perfect option when it comes to buying a bird. While that is certainly an option, you must make sure that the pet store endorses good care and ethical breeding of the birds. When you are looking for a lorikeet in a pet store, make sure that you look for the following:

- Clean cages
- Well-maintained birds
- Hygienic bird rooms that are away from the other animals being sold
- Clean food bowls and clean drinking water for the birds
- Knowledgeable staff
- Adequate quarantining of all the birds.

It is true that breeders are hard to find because they usually live in areas that are on the outskirts or because they do not invest much in advertising. That said, there are several websites that will list reputable breeders in your vicinity. You can also look for recommendations from other parrot owners or from a veterinarian in your locality.

If you are choosing a breeder from the Internet, especially, make sure that you visit their facility before you make any commitment. In any case, you must make sure you inspect the breeding conditions before you bring your bird home to avoid nasty surprises. There are a few advantages of seeking out a rainbow lorikeet breeder as opposed to buying from a pet store:

- You will be able to actually see the conditions and the environment that the birds are raised in.

- You will be able to see the parents of the bird to rule out any chances of genetic issues.

- With most reputable breeders, you will be able to find a lot of information and support with respect to raising your birds.

It is always an advantage to buy your bird from a breeder because, unlike a pet store, the birds do not come in in large lots from different facilities. When various birds from various locations are caged together, chances are that the risk of disease is very high. Breeders are also less expensive because they usually do not have to invest in large spaces, advertising and in hiring employees for their facility. This saving is passed on to those who buy from them.

What you need to know about pet stores
- While not all pet stores bring in their birds or other pets from pet factories, they are associated with breeders. You need to find out why the breeder did not sell the bird himself. You may find that the pet store owner breeds lorikeets or that they have a tie up with a breeder who does not have the time to make the sale.

  However, in most cases, breeders give up on the weaker birds and sell them off to pet stores. So, the low quality birds make their way in to the pet store.

- Pet store bought birds may have several individual problems. This can stem from the fact that they have not been hand tamed, they do not have the right environment to develop in or because they do not receive as much mental stimulation as required.

- These birds are not handled well when they are transferred from the aviary to the pet shop or from the pet shop to a new home. This causes a lot of issues.

- Pet stores are very noisy. In addition to that, they may not have enough light, the right diet or may be disturbed by too much handling by potential buyers.

- Birds are abruptly removed from their cage, separated from cage mates and then sent off to new homes. This is very stressful for these birds.

While these issues may not seem too serious to most of us, the fact is that lorikeets are very intelligent and highly cognitive. It is particularly important to make sure that these birds get the right care.

6. Adopting a Rainbow Lorikeet

There are several rescue shelters that are working consistently to make sure that birds that have been rescued or surrendered are able to find forever homes. They give you the option of fostering or adopting these birds.

With most of these organizations, a complete assessment of the family who will be taking the bird is mandatory to ensure that they are compatible. You will also be able to attend several in-house training programs that will educate you about providing proper care for the bird you bring home.

With these birds, their long life can be a bane. Some owners are unable to sustain the care that they provide or may just run out of patience with an adolescent rainbow lorikeet that is a little difficult to handle.

There are other birds that have been abandoned by breeders because they were unable to keep up with the demands of a stringent breeding program. Either way, a lorikeet does tend to become very lonely and can even develop mild to serious behavioral issues when they are abandoned. This is why it is very important to educate yourself about the bird before you decide to take one home, especially from a shelter.

Traits of a good shelter

Since the birds at shelters are already under a lot of stress, they need very good care. Without that, there are chances that the bird's condition will deteriorate with time. He may also contract several infections, as his immunity is compromised. With a good shelter, you will get all the support that you will need in order to raise your rescued bird correctly.

You can look for local shelters online. There are chances that you will find many of them in your vicinity. Here are some guidelines to help you choose a good shelter to adopt a lorikeet from:

- Every bird that is entered in this program should be checked thoroughly by an avian vet.

- Following that, the bird should be quarantined for at least 30 days off site. This means that the bird should be kept far away from the birds at the shelter.

- Once the bird has been removed from quarantining, it must be allowed to socialize with the volunteers and also with people who are looking to adopt.

- Facilities that provide a trainer are ideal, as they can help the bird work through various issues that are faced by the bird due to the transition and also abandonment.

- The facility should allow you to spend as much time as you need with the bird that you want to take home.

- If you are new to the world of parrots, the shelter should be willing to provide you with as much information as you need. In fact, with many facilities, there are regular classes that you are encouraged to attend before you choose to adopt a rainbow lorikeet.

The process of adoption

Each shelter will have its own unique set of rules for everyone who wants to adopt a bird from them. However, there are some general rules that apply to almost every facility that you choose to adopt a bird from:

- You will have to fill in an application form with all your personal details.

- Some facilities will require you to attend a minimum number of classes before you can become eligible for adoption. If the history of the bird demands more attention, you may be asked to take additional classes.

- You must spend some time bonding with the bird that you choose. In some facilities, a minimum of three visits is mandatory. You will not be allowed to handle the bird unless you have finished at least one class. You can only handle the bird when staff members are present. Therefore, it is best that you make an appointment before you visit your bird.

- A complete physical exam of the other birds in your home might be necessary. This must be done by a certified avian vet. The goal of these examinations is to rule out psittacosis before taking the new bird home.

- A home visit is a must with every facility. They will also need the cage to be approved. So, you will have to invest in the cage before the bird comes home. In some facilities, there is a restriction on how far the potential adopters can reside from the shelter.

- You will have to pay an adoption fee that ranges from $30-$100 or £15-£50 based on the medical attention or other care that the bird required while at the facility.

Only when you have completed all these procedures will you be allowed to take the bird home. Even then, there are some conditions that you need to guarantee to be eligible for adoption:
- You will not use the bird for any breeding purposes.

- The bird should never be taken out of the house without a cage or a harness at least.

- The bird should be kept in an environment that is 100% smoke free.

- The bird should be examined annually be a vet approved by the facility.

- The bird should be given a balanced diet that includes all the foods that are part of the natural diet of the rainbow lorikeet.

- You must allow follow up visits by the authorities at the facility.

- In case you are unable to keep the bird for any reason, it will be surrendered to the facility that you adopted it from.

These rescue shelters put in a lot of work with each bird that is rescued. That is why they are extra cautious about whom the birds are given to. Some of them will not let you have a bird if there are aggressive pets at home or even if there is a child at home who are is very young.

You also have a limitation on how many birds you can adopt each year. Even after all the work, they have the right to decline the application. If they do so, you can try again and make sure you fit into their criteria of a good adopter.

7. Are you really ready?

Once you have decided where you want to source your bird from, the next question to ask yourself is if you are really ready for the bird. If you think that the rainbow lorikeet is not as big a responsibility as other pets such as dogs or cats, think again. Here are a few questions that you should ask yourself before bringing a rainbow lorikeet home:

- Are you willing to make a lifelong commitment to the bird? Remember that they will live up to about 20 years. How do you see your life after these years?

- Will you be able to set aside time to prepare your bird's food everyday? Rainbow lorikeets have special dietary requirements that you need to take care of.

- Do you have the time to play and interact with your bird? How much time are you willing to give the bird each day where you take him or her out of the cage and engage in activities together?

- Can you afford to get the bird regular vet exams? You must be able to take the bird for an annual check-up even if he seems to be in perfect health.

- Do you have enough space in your home? A rainbow lorikeet is a medium-sized bird but they need a good housing area where they can flap their wings, play and rest. A small cage in a corner is definitely not an option.

- If you do get bitten by the bird, what will you do? If you are afraid of this, you must reconsider bringing a bird home. There may be some accidents, particularly with rainbow lorikeets. If that puts the bird at the risk of being abandoned, then you must reconsider bringing one home in the first place.

- Are you ready to clean the cage regularly? Never let the poop and other dirt build up on the floor, as the bird will always be at the risk of falling ill.

- Are you okay with getting some bird poop on the floor, couch, table or maybe your favorite shirt? It is possible to potty train the bird but until then, these accidents may happen.

- Is it okay for the bird to be noisy at times? Parrots of all kinds may get noise at dawn and dusk. This is their instinct. If you have neighbors who may complain, make sure that you have their consent. In addition to that, you and your family should be up for some noise and screeching from time to time.

- Is it mandatory for the bird to be able to talk? While rainbow lorikeets can be trained to learn a few words, their talking ability is not as great as other species of parrots. If you want a parrot that can talk very well, then the rainbow lorikeet is not the bird for you.

- Are you willing to make lifestyle changes? There are several things like air fresheners, Teflon pans, ceiling fans and scented candles in our homes that may be hazardous to the bird. Are you willing to make modifications and changes to make your house a safe haven for the bird?

Only when you have satisfactory answers to these questions should you bring a bird home. A beautiful and intelligent bird like a rainbow lorikeet must never be turned into a trophy. They need your time and attention just as much as every other pet does. So, once you make a commitment, you should be able to stick to it.

Chapter 3: When You Bring the Lorikeet Home

A change in environment can be really stressful for birds. So, when you decide to bring the lorikeet home, make sure that he only has a positive experience from the time he leaves the pet store or the breeders until he reaches your home.

This begins with ensuring that the bird has a good drive to your place. If the bird is being shipped, you need to be additionally cautious, as the bird can develop several health issues due to stress. This chapter tells you everything that you need to know about keeping the first few interactions positive.

1. Driving the bird home

A drive is a very unique experience for a bird. Most often, a bird will find this very stressful because of the moving objects, the colors and all the sights and sounds. This may seem very ordinary to you, but for a bird it can actually be very traumatic.

It is a good idea to purchase a temporary travel cage that you can even use in the future for vet visits. This will keep your bird secure throughout the drive. Place the cage securely on the seat and strap it in. Make sure that the floor is lined with paper or any other substrate. You also need to keep some treats and water available to the bird. If your breeder or pet store is able to give you one of the bird's toys it is a good idea, as he will have something familiar during this new experience.

Do not talk to the bird when you are driving home. It is a good idea to go individually and not as a group when you buy the bird. New human voices are very disturbing for the bird. If you go as a group, there will be several new voices that will stress the bird out even more. Make sure that you do not play any music throughout the drive. Basically, you will avoid any additional surprises for the bird.

Keep the air-conditioner on in the car and set it to room temperature. It could be slightly lower on a hot day. In case your home is a long drive from the breeder's, it is a good idea to take a break every half an hour. A ten-minute break is good enough for the bird to calm himself down and probably eat and drink a little. They may not even poop in a moving vehicle and become very uncomfortable if you do not give them a break.

2. When the bird is shipped

A breeder will not ship the bird to your doorstep. You will either have to collect the bird from the local post office or the airport. Remember that not all birds can be shipped through the postal service. It also depends on the regulations in your state. If your lorikeet has been shipped using a freight service, it is a lot more stressful, as the airport is busier and noisier than a post office.

Usually a bird is shipped within a week of making the payment. If the bird is being shipped with a freight service, you can ask for a specific date to collect your bird from the airport and he will be shipped accordingly. Once the bird has been shipped, you will be notified. You can contact the freight company to figure out how much time it will take for the package to arrive.

When you go to collect the box, you must take a small transfer cage along. The box will normally have a trap door. This will be marked with the words "live bird". Open this door and place it before the door of your bird's cage. Let the bird take its time to walk into the transfer cage.

When you are getting a bird shipped to your house, you will have to do a little bit of homework. Ask the breeder or the store what the bird is accustomed to eating. Make sure this food is available to the bird in large quantities when he arrives. Do not try to change the diet on the day he arrives, as he is already very stressed. You also need to give him clean drinking water using a bottle, preferably. Make sure the food and water is visible to the bird. Don't assume that he will go to the food if it is in the cage.

There are chances that your bird is sick, so you will drive him to the vet before you take him home. Make sure that he is certified as healthy. That way you will not have to worry about any critical illness in the future. During the bird's first drive with you, make sure you follow all the instructions given above.

In the case of death while shipping, you may contact your breeder. You will most likely not get a refund but it is good to inform him or her of the situation.

It is advised that you drive the bird home yourself. Look for a breeder who is closer to where you live. Even if it is a longer drive, it is safer for you to collect your bird. During the flight to your home, there are chances that the bird will come into contact with toxins, very hot or warm conditions, dust and other conditions that can severely affect his health.

3. When the bird arrives home

Like any other pet, you need to give your lorikeet some time to get used to the new environment. The switch is stressful. Therefore, keeping interactions minimal will help your bird immensely.

There are several things that you can do to make the first day of your lorikeet in your home comfortable. In fact, the first week is very important to help the bird create positive associations with his new space. If not, there are chances that he will take longer to build trust and bond with you and your family.

The first thing you need to do is make sure that the bird is allowed to calm down. You need to prepare his new enclosure. Place it in a room that is rather quiet. This room should be away from any main road where there could be a lot of noise due to traffic. The bird must feel secure, so place this cage against a wall. Do not keep it in an area like the hallway, as there is too much commotion. You definitely do not want to place it in the family room or the living room. The bird should be in a space that allows him to observe his new home and family without really getting in the middle of all the action.

Make plenty of food available for the bird. Keep fresh water in the cage too. The first day should not include any interaction. As a new pet owner, you may be excited to fondle and cuddle the bird, but this will only damage the health of your bird. Just walk past his cage, follow your normal routine but do not talk to him or interact with him.

You must make sure that you keep children away from the cage for the first few days. They will not tease or play with the bird. No loud music or television should be allowed in the house until the bird is at ease. You definitely do not want any visitors in your home. If there are any large and colorful objects in the room that you have placed the cage in, take it out immediately. If your home has multiple birds or other pets, you will not introduce them to the new bird. The new bird needs to be left alone.

It is a good idea to cover one part of the cage with a towel. This can become the bird's hiding place or sleeping area. It will also protect him from the light of the television and any other light in your home.

The next morning, you can simply change the food and water in the cage. Still do not talk to the bird. Just casually go about the cleaning and feeding and let your bird observe you. A bird that is already socialized will probably not be afraid of you. However, if your bird is reclusive and in one corner of the cage, he is probably still scared.

The most important thing to do would be to prepare your family and tell them that they will have to let the bird get acclimatized before they interact with the new member of the family. It is also a good idea to bring the bird home when you are in all day. Do not bring him if you know that he is going to be alone on a particular day. That will only scare him a lot more in this brand new environment. While there should not be any interaction, the bird should be able to watch and observe your family.

For the next week, try to talk as little as you can to your bird. Keep socialization to a minimum. This means that you will not host parties or have people over for at least one week after the lorikeet arrives. You also need to keep noises like the TV and radio at a minimum.

Make sure you pass by the cage often. That way, your bird will get accustomed to your presence. You will also be interacting with the bird when you are feeding him and cleaning the cage. This is the bonding time.

After a day or two, you can say words like "hello" and "bye" in a very soft and soothing voice. Once you think that the bird is ready, you can start actual interaction. You will know that your bird is ready by observing his body language. His posture will be erect, he will use the perch, and his level of activity will increase. In addition, when you approach the cage to feed him, he will not cover himself or retreat behind the towel. That indicates that your bird is getting used to your home.

Now, you can sit by the cage and talk to your bird in a calm voice. Just place your hands on the wall of the cage for a while and sit in front of the cage quietly. The bird will approach your hand, lick it and probably even nibble at it. This is a good sign, as it shows that your bird is not afraid of you. You can even move your hand around the walls and see if the bird follows your hand. If he does, he is warming up to you.

When you are interacting with your bird, make sure that you are at his eye level at all times. When you are feeding, cleaning or even just talking to him, stay at the same level as him. If you tower over the cage, he will view you as a predator and will get scared of you. He will also assume that you mean harm if he feels like you are much larger than him in size.

Staying at eye level, on the other hand, tells him that you are part of his flock and that you are both equals in the group. This will help him trust you more and approach you more positively.

4. Introducing your lorikeet to other pets

As mentioned before, lorikeets are extremely social creatures. Now, you may have a home with other birds or with other pets, or both. What is most important to make sure that your pets get along is to introduce them correctly.

That said, your pets may or may not get along with the new addition in your family. If there are any negative responses from the current house pet or from the rainbow lorikeet, keeping them apart is the best option.

Here are a few tips to make the interactions more positive.

Quarantining the new bird or birds

Before you get your birds to interact, the first thing you need to do is quarantine the new bird. That way, if the bird is carrying any diseases that can affect your aviary, you will be able to avoid this. Quarantining also ensures that your new bird does not develop any diseases due to interactions with your pet bird, which could be a carrier.

Quarantining is one of the biggest responsibilities of pet owners. This is the first step towards defending your old flock and your new bird from the possibility of any health issues.

When you have a flock that has been living together for a while, they would have developed a unique environment that keeps them immune to certain germs that they may be exposed to on a regular basis. Now, it does not matter how impeccable the living conditions of your new bird were when you bought him, it is necessary to quarantine the bird.

Why is quarantining so important? Remember that you have displaced the bird from its old ecosystem and have brought him to a new environment that may contain several germs that he has not been exposed to. This is another causal factor for the stress that birds experience when they are moved to a new location.

The stress can either be very minor or can be major based on the nature of the bird you bring home. When the bird is stressed, the immune system becomes weak. This means that the bird may not be as healthy as he was when you bought him.

If you fail to quarantine the bird, you are exposing him to a plethora of new germs that he may fall victim to. If the bird becomes ill, he will shed the pathogenic germ in large amounts. In addition to that, he will also shed any germ that he may have brought in from his previous home. That means that the environment in your home has several pathogens that your birds are probably not immune to.

Even if there are no new germs, the volume of the old ones can be so high that the birds are unable to handle it. While the new and the old bird may fall sick, it is obvious that we believe that the new bird is responsible for the illness.

The truth is that an improper quarantining procedure is the cause for this poor immune response. You are able to control the stress that the bird is going through and his ability to cope with the new home when you quarantine your birds correctly. With a gradual and small amount of exposure to the shared ecosystem of the birds, the new one and the existing flock will be able to build the immunity that they need.

Here are the correct steps to quarantine your bird so that they do not develop unwanted health issues. It does not matter if you are adopting the bird or fostering him temporarily, make sure that you do not neglect any steps:

- While a minimum of 30 days is recommended for quarantining, 6 weeks is the safe period to give the bird ample time to get used to the new environment.

- In this period, observe the bird carefully. There must not be any signs of illness such as lethargy, discharge from the eyes or beak, unusually colored droppings, watery droppings, etc.

- Watch the eating habits of the bird. When they are in a new environment, birds do find it traumatic and will stop eating. You may offer him some treats that he likes. Drinking water, eating and having a normal poop is mandatory for the bird.

- Bring home a gram scale that will allow you to weigh the bird on a regular basis. Sudden weight loss is a cause for concern.

- If your bird is unwell, take him to the vet immediately. You will have to quarantine him until he tests negative for the most common parrot diseases. This might be longer than six weeks.

- Even when the bird is stable and healthy, arrange for a vet visit halfway through the quarantine period.

- The room that you choose for your bird should be away from the rest of the flock. Only birds that are brought in on the same day, from the same place can be placed in the same quarantining room.

- The quarantine room should have enough fresh air and good natural light. Avoid rooms that have a furnace or an air conditioner. These are sources of stress for the bird.

- The most important thing to keep in mind is that birds tend to hide their illness, so do not place the bird with the rest of the flock unless he is checked by a vet, even if he seems perfectly healthy.

- It is a good idea to have an apron in the quarantine room that you will use when you are handling the new bird. Make sure that you remove this apron and wash your hands thoroughly before you handle your existing flock.

- When the quarantined bird is being given any medication, the syringe or the feeder that you use should be kept away from the housing area of the existing flock.

- Once the new bird has settled in and the quarantine period has come to an end, discard any object such as a perch or a toy that you cannot sterilize.

- The food and water bowls of the quarantined bird should never be washed along with those belonging to the existing flock.

When you are done with the internal quarantining, make it a habit to quarantine your birds from any external source of infection. If you visit the zoo, visit other birds or reptiles, it is recommended that you take keep the shoes that you have worn outside your home. The clothes that you have worn when you are visiting other birds should be washed and cleaned. Make sure that you wash your hands the moment you get home. This is true even if you are walking through a park that may have ducks or geese.
Our clothes and shoes can carry dander and droppings that will in turn carry several disease causing organisms. The more precaution you take, the safer your birds will be.

Introducing the birds properly
Introductions can begin by placing the new bird in a separate cage next to the cage of your existing bird or birds. If the birds respond with loud screeching and a lot of noise, let them be. They will settle down in a while.

Let them stay in the same room for a few days to get used to each other's presence. Then, you can try to make the introductions to your flock.

In your flock, there is an obvious pecking order. You will notice that one bird is the most dominant one of all and another one is most submissive. Allow the submissive bird to meet the new bird first. It is best that you let the birds out so that they are in neutral territory. If you put the submissive bird in the cage of the new one, he may get territorial and aggressive.

When these birds are comfortable in each other's presence, it is time to introduce the next bird in the order of dominance leading up to the most dominant one. In neutral areas, fights are less likely to happen. If they do occur, it is best that you put the birds back in separate cages.

When you have a mixed aviary, it is a good idea to keep birds that are similar in size together. The small bird can get really intimidated by a bird that is too large. You must also avoid housing birds that are closely related to prevent any chances of hybridization.

There must be additional feeding stations as well as water sources. In case one of the birds is very dominant and aggressive, he may control all the sources of food and water if there is just one available.

Separate the area within the cage using sleeping tents or plant covers. This will give the meek bird a place to hide in. Then, when you spot the problem, you will be able to help the bird in case he is unable to protect himself.

You may want to keep pairs of the same species to promote breeding. Avoid having more than one pair unless you plan to have a flock of the same birds.

The birds must be checked on everyday to see if there are any signs of fighting or chasing. The birds that are being attacked should be placed in a separate cage immediately.

Introducing rainbow lorikeets to other pets
If you have a cat or dog at home, ask yourself if you really want to introduce them without any barriers. It doesn't matter how gentle your cat or dog it, the sheer size difference is cause for concern when you are introducing a bird to your cat or dog.

You must also never forget that your cat or dog is a natural predator for a bird. This will make it extremely stressful for your rainbow lorikeet and may lead to stress-related issues like feather plucking if the interactions are not monitored.

The first thing you need to make sure is that the cage is in a part of the house that does not allow the cat or dog to climb over it. Even if the pet cannot reach in, this act itself can be traumatizing for the bird. It can also lead to accidents like the cage falling over, which will also put your pet at risk of injuries.

If you must introduce them, you can do so after the bird has settled into the new house. When they are able to interact with you without any signs of stress, it is time to introduce them to their furry pals.

Place the cage in a room that the pet spends most of his or her time in. Watch your bird's reaction and the reaction of the pet. If the response is violent in the form of loud barking or growling, put the bird back and let him relax. Do this a couple of times until the bird is not interesting to your pet anymore.

You will know this when you place the cage in the room and your cat or dog simply won't respond to the bird. Now, taking the bird out of the cage at this point is still not advisable unless you are fully ready.

For the bird to be let out of the cage, you must be able to handle him and pick him up in a jiffy in case there is a negative response from the pet towards the bird. If the bird has not been hand-tamed yet, you can certainly not let him meet the pet outside the cage.

You can try to get the bird and the pet to interact in any open area when you are supervising. If they are calm, then you can let them explore the new scents and sounds. However, while cat and dog bites are severely damaging to the bird, it has been reported that a threatened rainbow lorikeet has injured dogs and cats with a sharp bite or peck.

This is why you must always make sure that the bird is secure in the cage when you have to leave the house. Even if the interactions in your presence have been calm and relaxed, it does not mean that your pet and the rainbow lorikeet can be great buddies. If the instincts do kick in, you may come home to the most terrifying scene and you have no one to blame but yourself.

5. A few rules for the family

When you bring a bird home, you need to remember that the whole family is responsible for making the bird feel comfortable in your home. A few simple rules should be followed by every member of your family:

- The person who has brought the bird home will be the one doing most of the handling until the bird is used to the family. This includes feeding and watering the bird for the first few days.

- Children must be strictly told not to tease the bird or try to play with it. Rainbow lorikeets are birds that will bite when threatened. This is purely for the safety of your child.

- Do not leave brightly colored objects near the bird's housing area. This includes toys, clothes or any large item that can scare the poor bird.

- Verbal communication should be kept to a minimum with the new bird. The family must strive to keep the environment of the bird as calm and comforting as possible. This means that they will not show off the bird to friends until the bird is ready.

- No pictures with the bird. When you are trying to get a selfie with your new bird or are trying to take a picture of the bird, he becomes very aware of the fact that something is going on. Added to that, you may turn the flash on or the jazzy cover of your phone may scare the bird.

- The family will ease their way into the bird's heart. This will include just standing near the cage with the hands on the sides for a few minutes. Make sure the person is at eye level to prevent the bird from feeling like he is being attacked by a predator.

- No loud noises in the room that you have stationed your bird in.

With these rules, you will prevent any accidents with respect to the bird. Children, especially, should be taught to treat the bird with a lot of respect.

Chapter 4: Rainbow Lorikeet Care Guide

Proper care for your rainbow lorikeet requires a lot of preparation even before the bird is home. This chapter will take you step by step through correct rainbow lorikeet care.

1. Before the bird arrives

There are two things that you need to take care of before the bird is home: the housing and bird proofing.

Housing your rainbow lorikeet

Make sure that the housing area of the bird is fully set up before you bring him home. That will make the transition much easier. You can keep the bird in the permanent housing area from day 1 instead of adding to the stress of moving to a new cage just after the bird has gotten used to the new home.

Cage Specifications

Rainbow lorikeets are birds that love to play and move around, so it is necessary that you provide them with a large enough cage that allows them to do so.

For a rainbow lorikeet, the minimum size of the cage should be 24x24x20 inches. The cage should be wide enough to make sure that you can include as many accessories and toys as possible. The way to check if the size is good enough for your bird is that he should be able to stretch his wings in all directions without touching the bars of the cage.

In case you decide to keep a pair of birds, then you definitely need a larger cage. You also need to make sure that you have a spare cage in order to keep the birds separately in case one of them falls sick or if the birds show any aggression towards one another during the breeding season.

The cage can be lined with newspaper, as it is the safest option for a substrate. If you plan to use wood shavings, then avoid redwood, pine and cedar, as they give out certain hydrocarbons that are toxic. This can damage the respiratory tract of the bird. Aspen shaving is a good idea.

At the bottom of the cage, you can place a grate so that the droppings do not collect on the floor. However, sometimes when there are deposits on the grate that you will have to remove periodically. Otherwise, it will become uncomfortable for the bird to walk on the floor.

Never use any pine shavings, corncobs, walnut shells or cedar shavings on the floor as substrate. They can cause irritation to the bird and can even lead to some allergic symptoms. The best option is clean and dry grass, aspen shavings or non-toxic sawdust. If you are using wood chips, choose the larger ones so that the birds do not ingest them accidentally.

Newspaper, brown paper bags or paper towels are the best option to cover the floor. These materials are easy to change, provide best absorption and are also the most economical way to go when you have to monitor the droppings of your bird on a regular basis.

Avoid placing any food dish holders in your bird's cage, as the birds can get stuck in the openings of these holders. Even when you are snapping the feeder cups in, you should be careful as the wings can get stuck when you snap it in place. Even the toes and legs can get stuck when they are trying to eat. The best option is to place ceramic or plastic bowls of good quality on the floor of the cage. Birds may perch on the metal holders and can get seriously injured if the design is not up to the mark.

Using a water bottle or any other watering device is not necessary unless your bird has the habit of pooping in the water or dirtying the water with their feathers. The traditional watering dishes are the best option, as they are also easy to clean. This also ensures that the birds get to drink enough water. Dehydration must be prevented at all costs, as it is the leading cause for deaths in captive birds.

Cage accessories
You can make the cage a fun place for the bird to be in with a few accessories:

Perches
There are different kinds of perches that you can use for your birdcage. You may use ropes, as these are the easiest ones to install and can be fun for the bird. Apple wood, maple and madrone wood perches are the safest

option for birds. If you wish to use PVC, only choose plumber grade PVC, as it is safe for the birds. Only get an acrylic perch if it has been sanded on the surface. If the perch is too slippery, it will lead to issues with the bird's toes. Sand or concrete perches may be the best option, as they keep the nails of the bird trim and also let the bird sharpen its beak.

Toys

If there is one thing that rainbow lorikeets love to do, it is to play all day. They need adequate mental stimulation in order to be healthy and happy. This can only be achieved when you have enough toys for the birds. There are a variety of toys that you can include to keep the bird engaged all day long.

Rainbow lorikeets love to explore with their beaks. For this reason, they need to have toys that will last longer. The toys should also be sturdier in comparison to a toy that you may buy for a smaller bird like the rainbow lorikeet. It is best that you choose toys made from plastic or any acrylic material. You will be able to find exclusive shredding and chewing toys that are actually good for the birds.

Toys made from safe woods like aspen and birch will satisfy the chewing needs of the birds. There are also toys that are made from rope or any other digestive material that is safe, even if your bird accidentally swallows a few bits. Leather is also a great option when it comes to chewing toys. You can either mount or hang these toys as long as you keep all the safety aspects in mind.

What you need to ensure with toys that you buy for your rainbow lorikeets is variety. There should be a variety of textures, colors, shapes and sizes. These birds are extremely mentally active and will get easily bored with monotony. So, you must try to rotate the toys every week in order to keep them interested.

You can even move the toys around to provide some variety to the birds. You will know that your bird is bored of a certain toy when you see it lying in one end of the room without the bird even noticing it.

Observing your bird's playtime can give you a lot of clues about what he likes or dislikes. If he is fond of a certain type of toy and is inclined to playing with that more often, then you can bring in more varieties of that toy, maybe different textures and sizes.

For example, if your bird likes the swings then you can choose from a variety of swings made from wood, beads or rope. Having more than one type of the toy gives you the advantage of moving it around to keep your bird interested in it for longer.

Because your rainbow lorikeet is going to spend a lot of time with his toys, it is mandatory to take all the necessary precautions to keep him safe. The danger of getting entangled and suffocating is real with a rainbow lorikeet.

The issue of entangling is common with toys that are suspended. If the toy is suspended using a chain link, then you need to make sure that the link is large enough for the whole body of the bird to pass through or it should be so small that the bird cannot even get his toe through it.

The length of the suspended toy also matters a lot. You need to make sure that the length is not more than that which can wrap around your thumb once. If the length is too much, the bird can hang from it when entangled. If you notice that the exposed length is more than this, you can take precautions by either tying knots or by tying other small trinkets along the length of the twine or rope.

You need to make sure that any toy or perch that has ropes or twines attached to it does not have any fray that can wrap around the toe of the bird. In many cases, the toes of the bird will get entangled and can actually break or tear.

The attachment that you use for the toy is also very important. The most dangerous one for the beak of the bird is the split ring or the key ring. These rings are easily opened by the bird using the beak. Then, you have the risk of the ring going through the beak or the risk of the beak getting stuck in it. Even with carabineers, the beak of the bird can get mutilated.

The best option to suspend the bird's toys is a C-clasp. The screw type closing mechanism will reduce any chance of the beak getting trapped in it. Pinching of the beak or the toe is also less likely to occur with these clasps.

It is true that the rope type or suspended type of toys pose the biggest risk for a rainbow lorikeet. However, you must never neglect the small foot toys. These toys may have small parts that are likely to break and cause choking in case the bird swallows it accidentally.

Non-natural parts of any toy that you think can be chewed up or bitten will pose the serious threat of intestinal blockage in case it is swallowed accidentally.

You can get really creative with the toys. Making foraging toys using paper and treats is a great idea. You can even recycle an old toy as long as you keep the safety measures in mind. Now, if your bird has destroyed a toy completely, it is a sign that he has thoroughly enjoyed it.

Where to place the cage

Where you put the cage will also matter in keeping the bird comfortable in the cage. Here are a few pointers that will help you with this:

- The cage should be kept in a quiet spot in the house, free from any distraction. A corner wall is the perfect place with the cage resting against the wall. This will make the bird feel very secure.

- The bird must be able to see the activities in your household from his cage. If he is secluded, then he can be easily startled. Rainbow lorikeets learn everything about their new home through observation. So, you can keep him in a corner that allows him to see you and your family for the most part. Yet, he must not be right in the middle of all the action, as it will become a little stressful for him.

- The cage should be away from noise, so a room that is facing a road with too much traffic is not the best idea. He will always be alert and can even get frightened with the noise during the day or the lights of the vehicles zipping around at night.

- The area around the cage also matters. Make sure that there is no cemented surface or concrete surface near the cage. This will increase the chance of serious injuries should your bird accidentally fall out of the cage or fall when he is let out of the cage.

- The cage must be away from the air conditioner, heater and the kitchen. Sudden fluctuations of temperature and the fumes from these areas can lead to health issues such as respiratory problems. It will also stress the bird out, which will lead to behavioral issues like plucking of his feathers.

- Ample light is necessary for birds from the tropical areas. If you live in an area that does not allow the bird to get a lot of natural light, you must provide the bird with a full spectrum artificial light. This is crucial in the development of the bird as it keeps his body clock aligned.

The placement of the cage is crucial in helping your bird make an easy transition into your home. The more opportunity he has to retreat and rest, the easier it will become for him to adjust to his new home and all the members of his new flock.

Ensuring safety
It is not enough that your cage is large and well equipped with accessories. It is necessary to make sure that your bird is safe in the cage. Here are some safety measures that you can take to keep your bird safe in the cage:

- Choose a rectangular cage as opposed to a round one. In the case of round cages, the birds do not have anywhere to hide or retreat into when they are scared. These cages will also affect the feathers of the bird, especially the ones on the tail.

- It is best that you choose a powder-coated or stainless steel cage. Others that are made of wrought iron or with a painted surface can be dangerous, as they may have deposits of zinc or lead.

- The bars should be parallel all over the cage. They must not converge anywhere.

- The distance between two bars must be appropriate. The width must be such that the bird is not able to fit his head through them and should not be so small that the toes get stuck.

- Make sure that the bars are made of a strong enough material to withstand the bite from your rainbow Lorikeet, who will use his beak to climb up and down.

- If you are using any towels or covering material on the cage, then you should make sure that there are no threads or holes in them. This may lead to strangulation or may have the bird's toenails or legs entangled, leading to fractures or injuries.

- The cage should not have any protrusions or sharp edges. If your bird scrapes his body on these protrusions, it can lead to severe injuries that may cause infections.

With these tips, you can be sure that your birdcage is perfect for your rainbow lorikeet.

Bird proofing

Your home should be a safe environment for your bird. That can be achieved when your home is bird proofed to prevent any chances of injury or accidents in your home. Here are some useful tips to bird proof your home:

- Make sure that the cage is not placed on a hard surface. Should your bird have a fall, he can sustain serious injuries.

- The windows should be marked or should have a safe object hanging in front of it. That way, you will not have any instance of the bird flying into the windows and hurting himself.

- Electrical wires should be enclosed completely. There should not be any loose wires near the cage, especially on the floor. If someone accidentally trips on it and tips the cage over, it can be bad news for your bird.

- All the toilet lids and any water container in your home should be covered. There have been several reports of lorikeets and other species of birds drowning accidentally.

- The cage should be away from the kitchen. There are fumes, especially those released by Teflon pans, which can be toxic for your bird. Prolonged exposure to these fumes can cause serious health issues.

- It is best to have a kitchen with a door that can be closed every time the lorikeet is out of the cage. Hot stovetops and utensils are the number one cause of injuries in birds.

- Do not have doors that can close automatically. There are chances that your bird will get caught in between when the door is shutting.

- Table fans should be kept out of the bird's way. Make sure that all fans, table or ceiling, are off when your bird is let out of the cage.

- Always check doors and windows when you leave your home. You do not want your bird to get away if you leave the house with one of them open.

- Make sure you check if a certain plant is toxic to your bird or not when you place it near the cage of the bird.

- The cage doors should have a secure lock. A simple latch does not hold a lorikeet back, as they will soon figure out how to let themselves out. Do not forget that you are dealing with a very intelligent bird.

The safer the environment, the less stressed your bird will be. You will also not have to worry about untoward incidents that will leave your bird with serious injuries. Even after all the precautions have been taken, make sure that you never leave the bird out of his cage without proper supervision.

2. Feeding rainbow lorikeets

The care that you provide once the bird is home determines the health of the bird overall. There are some aspects to rainbow lorikeet care that are quite different. Learning more can help you keep the bird healthy and happy even if you do not have any experience with rainbow lorikeets.

Unlike other species of true parrots, rainbow lorikeets do not consume seeds and pellets. In the wild, these birds feed on nectar, fruits, vegetables and pollen. They have brush-like tongues that help them maintain this unique diet. They usually consume nectar from flowers like grevilleas and bottlebrush.

You will be able to find foods that have been specially formulated for these birds in most pet stores. You can additionally provide fresh fruit as supplements. These foods give them the nutrients that they need to survive.

The best option is to give your lorikeet orange veggies like pumpkin, carrot or sweet potato. In addition to that, you can give your lorikeet the following:

- Beans
- Apples
- Broccoli
- Apples
- Melon
- Mango
- Grapes
- Parsley
- Spinach
- Sweet corn
- Strawberries
- Pears.

You can also give your lorikeet rice and pasta. You can give them sprouted seeds. It is a good idea to puree the fruits or the other foods that you are giving your bird. You can also slice them up finely. However, fruit alone should not be the major component of your bird's diet.

Use one or two fruits at a time. Mixing them up will give your bird a good variety. You must also make sure that you do not leave any pureed fruit or veggies in the cage for too long, as it spoils quite easily.

In the wild, the native fruits that lorikeets eat contain more fiber and protein in comparison to the fruits that are available to us. When the fiber is higher, the food transits through the gut slowly. Since lorikeets tend to digest proteins poorly, this slow movement of food allows better absorption of any protein that they get through their food.

If you want your lorikeet to have a "natural" diet, bottlebrush, eucalyptus and callistemon branches can be included in the diet. You can also provide juice from fruits like peach and apple.

Make sure you give the formulated feed and the puree separately to the bird. Mixing them up can lead to fermentation and growth of bacteria. Watch the eating habits of the bird. If you notice that food is left over everyday, you can reduce the portion slightly.

There are some recommended formulated foods for rainbow lorikeets such as:
- Harrison's Bird Food
- Wombaroo Lorikeet and Honeyeater Food
- Dr.Mac's Organic Origins for Lorikeets
- Vetafarm Blossom Nectar
- Vetafarm Golden Lori Dry Nectar.

You can add recommended supplements to your bird's diet to make sure that they get adequate nutrients.

What not to feed Lorikeets
These birds cannot digest any animal protein. This includes eggs. This food can be toxic to the birds. In addition to that you must also avoid:
- Avocadoes
- Coffee or anything containing caffeine
- Alcohol
- Pits of fruits
- Chocolate
- Dairy products.

How much to feed the lorikeet
The amount of food that you give your lorikeet depends on several factors such as:

- Age: An older lorikeet will require less food in comparison to one that is still growing.

- Gender: The quantity and calcium requirement is higher in the case of females that are laying eggs.

- Behavior: If the bird is in a small cage, he will need less food, as he gets less exercise.

- Environment: A bird that is kept indoors will require less food than one in an outdoor aviary. The requirement of food can also change with temperature. It increases in colder temperatures, as the bird needs more energy to maintain body temperature. If it is a multi-bird aviary, the food requirement is higher, as the birds are more active.

- The season: When your rainbow lorikeet is molting, the food requirement is higher.

- Health: Birds that are ill will eat less. The nutrient requirement will also change if your bird is undergoing any treatment.

Since the food consumed by lorikeets has a high water concentration, they do not need as much drinking water. However, you need to make sure that fresh and clean water is available to your bird at all times.

On average, you should feed your lorikeet 14kg per day, once or twice a day. You should change the feed every day, as food left out for too long can rot and cause illness in the bird.

Signs that the diet is poor
There are some signs that will tell you that the bird is not getting the right nutrients:

- The loss of feathers is excessive even when it is not molting season.

- The feathers change colors. The coloration of the feathers of lorikeets is due to several nutrients like vitamin A, E and C, selenium, zinc, carotenoids and amino acids.

- The bird is lethargic

- The bird's vocalization changes drastically.

If you see any of these signs, you can consult your vet to provide better feeding options for your bird.

3. Grooming rainbow lorikeets

Grooming is one of the most essential parts of bird care. Normally, they groom themselves by preening their feathers and tucking them into place. They will use the water from their bowls to wet their feathers and keep them clean. There is a certain gland called the uropygial gland that secretes oil, which helps keep your bird's feathers waterproof. The bird will pick this oil up with his beak and smooth it over his feathers. However, there are some grooming activities that you need to engage your bird in. This is also a great bonding activity for you and your bird.

Bathing

Rainbow lorikeets require regular bathing in order to stay healthy. They love to splash around in water. They may even take a dip in their water bowl once in a while to keep themselves cool. But, you need to make it a point to give your bird a bath every 15 days in order to keep his feathers clean and free from any matting.

You need not use any soap on your bird unless there is any debris or dirt on the feathers. It is a good idea to consult your vet before using a certain soap on your bird. Some of them may have chemicals that are toxic for your bird. Use soap locally on the area that is dirty and rinse it gently with warm water.

The best way to bathe your bird is to mist his feathers. If he enjoys it, he will lift his feathers and move around allowing you to continue. On the other hand, if he begins to crouch or back away, it means that he does not like it. Never spray directly in the bird's face.

You can also use a shallow water bath to let your bird take a dip. Let the bird step up on your finger, then lower your hand until the bird just touches the water a little. If your bird wants to take a bath, he will hop in. If you want to urge him to take a bath, you can also put some spinach leaves in the water. The bird will hop in and chew on the seeds while taking a bath.

Some people also place a perch under the shower to mimic rainfall and let the bird take a bath.

Wing Clipping
It is never advisable for first-time owners to clip the wings of the bird themselves. You must make sure that you consult your vet and learn how to do this before you try it on your bird. If not, two things can happen: you could cut a blood feather, causing profuse bleeding, or you could clip the wings unevenly. Your bird relies on his wings to get his balance. If they are not clipped properly, he will try to even them out himself, plucking the feathers out in the process. If this becomes a habit, it will turn into a behavioral problem.

If you want to clip the wings at home, you need to only cut the first three primary feathers. These are the first three longest feathers on the wing. Pick your bird up using a towel. Now, hold him on your thigh face down. Wrap him in the towel, exposing only the wing that is to be clipped, and of course his head. Spread the feathers out and cut out 1 cm from each of the three primary feathers. Do the same on the other side. Then, open out both the wings and examine them to be sure that they are even.

If you cut a blood feather accidentally, stop the bleeding immediately using a styptic pencil or cornstarch. Then, hold it down with a piece of clean gauze.

Beak and toe trimming
This grooming process is optional. If you notice that your bird's toes and beak are getting stuck in the toys or any fabric, you can trim them to avoid any accidents. If the beak or toe of your bird is stuck to the fabric on your sofa and he tries to move suddenly, there are chances that the whole toe rips off or the beak is severely damaged. To avoid this, trim the sharp ends.

Wrap the bird with a towel, only exposing the part that you want to trim. In the case of the beak, gently lift the upper mandible with your finger and feel the sharp end. Keep the beak supported and trim the beak using a nail file. When you feel that it is just blunt, stop trimming. If the nail or the toe is too short, the bird will be unable to climb and hold properly.

Even with the toe, make sure that you have a finger supporting the nail you want to trim to avoid any chances of breakage or unwanted damage.

Remember that bonding with a bird as intelligent as the rainbow lorikeet requires a lot of effort from your end. These birds will analyze every situation that they are put in and even the slightest doubt will break their trust. If you have adopted a bird that has been abused, this will take longer. You will also need a lot of assistance from your avian vet to gain the trust of such birds. Take it one step at a time and make sure that you do not rush him.

4. Cage Maintenance

Rainbow lorikeets are extremely messy birds, so you need to do some routine cleaning such as washing the food and water bowls and changing the substrate on a regular basis. You can even make a schedule to clean your bird's cage regularly.

Daily cleaning

When you feed your birds every day, ensure that you check the cage thoroughly. Here are a few practices that are recommended for daily cleaning.

The food and water bowls

- Before you feed the bird, clean the bowls thoroughly. Rinse the bowls first and then lather them with soap. The soap must be washed off entirely. After the bowl is clean, towel it dry with a towel that is clean.

- Check if the dishes are dishwasher safe. In case you are planning to put them in the dishwasher, they must be suitable for it.

- The detergent that you use for cleaning must be animal safe. You can find several such options at the local pet store. If not, you will even be able to find them online or in stores that sell organic and natural products.

- It is always a good idea to have extra bowls for days when you may not have time to clean the bowls thoroughly.

Check the cage accessories
- Needless to say, you will have several perches and toys in the cage. If you notice that they have any dirt or droppings on them, you must clean them out thoroughly.

- The accessories are cleaned in the same manner as the dishes. Use animal friendly soap to lather up and then scrub them well. Using warm water is a good idea to disinfect these accessories a little better.

- When you put the toys back in the cage, you may want to move them around to give your bird some stimulation.

Cleaning the substrate or lining
- Replacing the cage lining material is a must. The best option available is paper lining available in stores or newspaper. These options are safe, easy to clean and economical.

- The old liner must be removed fully each day and the surface beneath it should be wiped with a rag or sponge to remove the paper that may be stuck on the floor.

- It is necessary that the lining material is free from any colored ink, as these pigments can be toxic to your bird.

- The general rule is to have seven layers of paper at least. That way it is completely absorbent and you will have fewer pieces sticking to the floor.

When you are doing the daily cleaning, it is ok for the bird to stay in the cage. However, if you have had cases of the bird flying out of the cage, it is best that you keep him in a separate cage when you are doing so. You may use a travel carrier as a temporary option when you are cleaning the cage.

Weekly or monthly cleaning

You can set the schedule for cleaning the cage based on the number of birds that you have. The higher the number of birds, the more often you have to clean. The size of the cage also matters. If the cage is smaller, it will have to be cleaned more frequently. With birds like rainbow lorikeets that are medium sized, you can plan a fortnightly schedule as well, as they are less likely to mess the cage up.

There are some simple steps that will help you be more organized when cleaning the cage:

- The first thing is to get all your supplies in place. You will need the following to clean your bird cage completely:
  - Cage liners
  - Cage wipes and paper towels
  - Sandpaper
  - Scrub brush or an old brush.

- The bird must be kept in a safe cage or travel cage. It is best that you place the bird in another room in order to keep the fumes from the cleaning supplies away from the bird.

- All the toys and accessories must be removed from the cage.

- If you notice seeds on the floor or any loose droppings, get rid of them as well. The floor must be scrubbed hard with soapy water. Make sure that the soap is mild. It is also possible to place the cage in a large tub and then wash it with a hose. You can then spray the interiors with a disinfectant solution.

- Once you have washed the cage, it should dry completely before you place the accessories back. Air drying in the sun is the best option.

- The perches and toys should be cleaned completely to get rid of any debris or droppings. Rinse the accessories well before you apply any disinfectant on them. Some of these perches made from plastic or wood may also be safe to wash in the dishwasher. You can put the ropes and softer toys in the washbasin.

- The toys and accessories must be fully dried before they are placed back in. You can air dry them in the sun. If you do not have the time for it, you can even dry them in an oven.

- If you have two sets it is easier to manage the cage. Any toy or perch that is broken or frayed must be removed as it may lead to injuries.

- Once you have cleaned the cage, the next step is to clean the area around the cage. You may vacuum the area or even opt to wash and disinfect it. The area under the carpet should be cleaned fully too.

- Line the cage with new substrate, add fresh food and water and also put in all the dry items back into the cage.

It is also a good idea to clean the areas that the bird plays in and the travel cage to maintain complete hygiene for the birds.

The right disinfectants

Using safe disinfectants is just as important as cleaning the cage. You need to ensure that it is effective but at the same time is not harmful or toxic to your bird.

Birds are very sensitive to toxic fumes and you must choose very carefully. Here are a few tips about using disinfectants in the cage:

- The disinfectant must be potent enough to get rid of fungi, bacteria and viruses without harming the bird.

- There are many options available for you to choose at pet stores. However, the best option and most readily available one is household bleach. You can make a dilute solution of ½ cup of bleach in about a gallon of water.

- Remember that any organic material such as seeds or droppings must be removed completely before you use a disinfectant in the cage. They normally hinder the solution from working properly. The areas that have been soiled should be cleaned thoroughly with hot water mixed with a dishwashing solution. Then you can rinse thoroughly before you spray the disinfectant.

- The disinfectant must be allowed to dry for at least ten minutes after it is applied onto a surface. Then you will rinse it with water. If you choose to use bleach solution, do so in an area that is well ventilated.

- Your safety is also very important and you must wear rubber gloves and safety goggles when you are cleaning the cage.

- The cage items must dry fully before placing them back. Any presence of moisture will make it a breeding ground for microbes.

If you are unsure about the disinfectant that you should use, you may ask your vet to provide you with the right options to clean the cage. In the case of any health issue, the vet may provide you with medicated cage cleaners as well.

Chapter 5: Bonding With The Rainbow Lorikeet

Bonding with your rainbow lorikeet is extremely essential. This is how you can keep the bird healthy and mentally stimulated. Besides providing your bird with toys, you can also make your interactions with the bird better for better health.

1. Is your bird bonding with you?

There are several signs that your rainbow lorikeet is bonding with you. Sometimes, this can go overboard, leading to over-bonding. This is the root of several issues like biting in these birds, so the question is whether the bond with your bird is healthy or not.

What are the signs of bonding?

From the time you bring the bird into your home, you will notice that he slowly warms to you and your family. Then, the bonding process progresses to a point when you are able to keep your bird on your shoulder and go about your daily activities. Let us take a look at the signs that show you that your bird is bonding with you.

Warming up: The initial stage
- Your bird will stop other activity and watch you when you are in the room or when you are passing by the cage. He will not be scared or nervous, however.

- He will follow your movements and will respond to your talking with different vocalizations.

- The bird moves towards you when you approach the cage.

- When you offer food from your hand, the bird eats it calmly.

The Progression: After the bird is "hand-tamed"
- He will step up onto your finger and will also let you pet him.

- He will call out to you when you are not around and he misses you.

Chapter 4: Caring for your Rainbow Lorikeet

- He may climb on your hand or shoulder, even when you do not ask him to.

The bond: Your bird loves you
- He will preen and groom your hair.

- He will not resist grooming activities like bathing or wing clipping. He will even let you hold him in awkward positions such as being upside down.

- He begins to trust you completely and even displays mating behavior such as regurgitation of food when you are around.

Signs of over-bonding
- The bird becomes very angry and aggressive when you talk to anyone else, especially another bird. He will scream and will even tear his toys apart.

- He is only happy if you are around and will always groom your hair or will try to feed you and display courting behavior. When you are gone, he will scream, become very scared or will just be depressed.

- The bird will not allow anyone else to handle him or touch him except the person he has bonded with.

- If any other person receives a slight bit of attention from the one he has bonded with, he will attack and bite them.

- The bird is extremely defensive about the person he is bonded with. If anyone tries to even touch the human he has bonded with, he will bite them. He will also attack other pets around your home.

- He will not let anyone else feed him.

Chapter 4: Caring for your Rainbow Lorikeet

Having an over-bonded bird can be very difficult. You will not be able to travel and leave the bird in someone else's care. He is also a potential threat to everyone around your home, especially children. The only way to prevent over-bonding is by properly training your bird and socializing him. This is not a difficult thing to do with rainbow lorikeets.

2. Understanding lorikeet body language

One of the most important aspects of bonding with any pet is understanding the body language. Since animals and birds do not communicate verbally, you have to watch the slightest change in their body language to understand what they are trying to tell you. Here are some common gestures and signs that you need to become aware of:

- **Flashing the pupils**: Parrots can control their pupils. If they dilate them, it is an indication of pleasure, anger or nervousness. You need to examine the surroundings of the bird to understand what this "pinning" or "flashing" signifies.

- **Tongue clicking**: This is a sign of pleasure and is often an invitation to you to come and play with him.

- **Beak clicking**: A sharp clicking sound made from the beak shows that your bird is feeling threatened. There could be some object or person in the room that the bird is scared of. He will additionally raise a foot and also extend his neck almost as if he is defending the cage.

- **Beak grinding:** You will hear the bird grinding his beak mostly at night. This is a sign of satisfaction and security.

- **Beak wiping**: When the bird is in an aviary, this is a sign of defense against the other birds or a warning sign. If your bird is alone and displaying this behavior, he is trying to get something out of his beak.

- **Regurgitation**: This behavior is displayed for their mates. Usually, a bird will regurgitate food and feed the contents to its partner. This is just what he is trying to do if he has a strong bond with you.

Chapter 4: Caring for your Rainbow Lorikeet

- **Head snaking**: If your bird moves the head from side to side almost like he is dancing or waving the head, he is trying to get your attention. The bird will even tilt his head to one side and look at you as a sign of interest towards what you are doing.

- **Lowering the head**: The bird will pull his wings close and lower the head and will almost look like he is about to fly. This is his way of telling you that he wants to come to you.

- **Beak fencing:** This is only seen when there are multiple birds in the cage. The birds will hold each other's beak almost like they are jousting. It is considered to be some sort of sexual behavior.

- **Panting:** If your bird is overheated or is too exhausted, then panting is observed. It is basically a sign of discomfort.

- **Wing drooping:** This is normal in young birds. If your bird is an adult, then it is a sign of illness.

- **Wing flipping:** A sharp flip or flick of the wing shows displeasure. It could also mean that your bird is just trying to set his feathers in place.

- **Quivering:** If the body or wings quiver, it is a sign of distrust. Talk to such a bird in a calm and comforting voice.

- **Marching:** If the bird marches with his head down, he is being defensive or aggressive. On the other hand, if his head is up, he is inviting you to play with him.

- **Tail bobbing:** This is usually a sign of sickness or fatigue, especially when the tail bobs when your bird is breathing.

- **Tail wagging:** When the bird sees his favorite person or toy, he wags his tail as a sign of happiness.

- **Tail fanning:** This is a dominant or aggressive behavior that basically tells you to back off.

Chapter 4: Caring for your Rainbow Lorikeet

- **Barking:** The bird is not mimicking another pet in your home. This is a natural vocalization that is meant to show dominance.

- **Purring:** If the bird's body is relaxed when he is purring, it shows contentment. However, if the body is still and the pupils are dilated, it is a sign of aggression.

- **Whistling, Talking and Singing:** These vocalizations tell you that your bird feels secure and safe. These are signs of a very happy bird.

- **Chattering:** You will hear the bird chattering or mumbling. He is only making his presence felt and is trying to get your attention.

3. Training rainbow lorikeets

Rainbow lorikeets are extremely intelligent creatures. This makes them highly responsive to training. This is also a great way to prevent any behavioral issues in your bird such as over-bonding.

Building trust

The first thing you want to accomplish with your bird is trust. This is a slow process but once you have managed it, it can be extremely rewarding. Start by just spending a few minutes every day talking to the bird and just placing your hand on the walls of the enclosure.

If you are the one feeding him every day, he is likely to bond faster. If your bird begins to respond by approaching your hand, licking it or nibbling at it slowly, it is a good sign. You can then start offering treats through the bars of the cage. If your bird does not eat it, just leave it in the cage and keep trying. Once the bird accepts a treat from your hand, the next step is to let him out of the cage.

Just open the cage door and let the bird come out. He will probably climb up on the cage and just explore the space around. Make sure that the space is safe for your bird and free from threats like pets or ceiling fans.

Then, you can hold out some treats in your hand and see if the bird will approach your hand. When your bird starts eating comfortably from your hand, it means that he is tamed enough to start the actual training.

Chapter 4: Caring for your Rainbow Lorikeet

Putting the bird back is easy. Just leave a few of his favorite treats or toys in the cage and he will go to them. In case your bird is reluctant to go into the cage before he is hand-tamed, use toweling to handle him. Wrap his body in a thick towel and let the ends fall over your hand. Then, pick him up gently holding the wings down and put him back in the cage. Treats and toys will help him understand that the cage is a fun place to be in.

Step up training

When a bird is ready to step up on your finger or hand, it means that he trusts you completely. Now, step up is more than a trust building command. Your bird must be able to step up in case of any emergency. If there is a natural calamity or if the bird is in danger and is unable to fly, stepping up will really help him get out of a dangerous situation.

You can begin the step up training with target training. Use a stick with a treat on the end and hold it through the cage, close to the bird. He may bite at it immediately. If not, gently touch the bird's beak with the stick. This stick is called the target. Once the bird understands that every time you present the target, he is going to get a treat, he will begin to look forward to it. He will even bite at it when there is no treat on the end.

Slowly start moving this target along the cage walls. If your bird follows it, it means that he is target trained. Now, open the door of the cage and hold the target there. The bird will start to come out of the cage following the target. When he does this, give him a treat. Do this a couple of times until he knows that getting out of the cage calls for a treat.

Then hold your finger horizontally in front of the cage and the target just behind the finger. When the bird is out of the cage, say "step up" and hold the finger steady. The bird may nibble at your finger as a way to make sure that it is safe to climb up. Do not withdraw the finger or move it, as the bird will lose trust. If the bird does step up, praise him abundantly and give him a treat. Slowly the bird will step up even without the target or treat. This is when he is fully bonded with you and trusts you completely.

You can later encourage him to step up on your shoulder or your head using the same technique. Once the bird is ready to step up on your shoulder, you can include him in all your daily activities and make the bond stronger.

Chapter 4: Caring for your Rainbow Lorikeet

Putting the bird back in the cage might become challenging. This is because he views this as an unpleasant experience as he will have to go away from you. So, place his favorite treats and toys in the cage after putting him back as an indication of the fun times ahead. Then, the bird will learn to stay by himself and keep himself entertained when put back in the cage. If not, he may develop separation anxiety and scream whenever you go away.

Toilet training

This is very important for lorikeets given the diet and their pooping habits. It may take some time but is certainly not impossible. When you are talking your bird all over the house with you after step up training, the last thing you want is your furniture and carpet to be covered with poop. You need to tell your bird that he can poop only in an assigned place and not anywhere else in the house. The first step is to help him understand that his cage is a good place to do his business.

You can start doing this with the first poop of the day. In the morning, when you are feeding the bird and cleaning up the bowls, place a fresh newspaper under the perch and wait for the bird to poop. Watch his body language when he does this. Knowing the changes in the body is very useful in further training. When he poops, praise him and give him a treat. That tells him that pooping in the cage is a good thing.

Usually, when birds poop, they tend to crunch their bodies and hold it stiff. Other birds may have other changes in the body language. When you begin to step the bird up and walk around your home with him, watch out for these signs. The moment you see this you can put a tissue under the bird and let him go about his business. When he does poop on the paper, praise him. If he poops elsewhere, don't react. No reaction is worse than reprimanding for a bird.

He will eventually learn that pooping on paper is good. You can then step the training up and hold the paper over a bin or inside the cage. When the bird uses this designated place, praise him and give him a treat. He will slowly understand that every time he needs to poop, he will have to go to the bin or to the cage in order to keep you happy.

The diet of the rainbow lorikeet makes them poop around the clock. This means that there are chances of accidents. Be patient and do not reprimand the bird unnecessarily. Instead, until your bird is fully potty trained, keep the expensive carpets and rugs away.

4. Working through behavioral issues

The three issues that most bird owners face are screaming, chewing and biting.

Biting

Since the beak of the rainbow lorikeet is soft, the bite does not hurt as much. However, it is no excuse to allow the bird to continue with this habit as it can really hurt a child or another pet in your home. For starters, you must understand what makes your bird bite and remove the stimulus to see a notable change.

Why birds bite

There are several things that will make your rainbow lorikeet react by nipping your hand. Here are a few common causes for biting:

- The way you approach your bird is very important. If you are feeling anxious or nervous, it is not a good idea to pick the bird up or approach him. That will induce bad behavior in the bird, as they are very sensitive to how we are feeling. They do not really think about biting and will only do it as a reflex.

- The bird may have learnt to associate your hands with something negative. When you use your hands to punish the bird by shooing them away or by throwing something at them, they will learn to react by biting. The best way to stop your bird from doing something is to redirect the attention with a toy.

- You use your hands only when you are taking the bird in and out of the cage. Sometimes, when the bird is not calm, they may make the association of the hand with unwanted touching or petting. Try other options like perches and play with the bird when he is out on a perch. Even when you pick the bird up, you may want to walk around or do

Chapter 4: Caring for your Rainbow Lorikeet

something fun that makes the bird think of your hand as a positive thing.

- The bird may be reacting to defend himself. If you have adopted a bird, he may have had a history of being beaten or threatened. Even when you make sudden movements with your hands and startle the bird, you will stimulate him to bite you.

- When you are approaching your bird, do it gently and without any jerks. The calmer you are and the more used to your hand the bird gets, the more he will respond to your hand positively. When the bird gains trust, you will notice that his nipping transforms into a more playful one as opposed to one that is very forceful.

- Putting the bird back in the cage is stressful for him and the bite may be a sign of protest when he does not want to go back in. You can make this more pleasant by putting some of your bird's favorite food in the cage before putting him back. Engaging in play or walking around before putting him back will also help. The less predictable you make this, the easier it is for you and your bird.

- Putting your bird back in the cage as punishment is the worst thing you can do. Then the cage becomes a place that the bird does not want to go into. Then, he will learn to fight you every time you try to put him back.

- Sometimes, a bird will hold your finger with his beak as a form of play. This is not painful. However, when you try to free your finger, the bird may dig in more. The best way to release your finger is to hold the bird with the other hand and pull him away gently. You can even redirect the bird using a toy or a perch that he may like to chew.

- Birds can become territorial at times, leading to this behavior. This may require you to change your approach to your bird a little. Try to get a cage that will allow you to change food and water bowls from the outside. You must also let the bird come out of the space using a target before you handle him. That way he is in a neutral territory and is less likely to bite.

- Your bird may be hormonal and may begin to bite people he perceives as competition. Then you can reduce the interaction of that person with the bird. You can even ask your vet for medicines to balance the hormones if you do not intend to breed your bird. Limiting daylight hours can also help you manage hormone-related biting.

Preventing bites
As discussed in the previous section, your bird will give you signs when he is about to bite. Understanding your bird's body language will help you retreat in time before you are bitten. If someone else is handling your rainbow lorikeet or is playing with him, you can take the bird away when he shows the signs of biting.

The best way to prevent biting is to hand-tame your bird. This will help your bird trust you more and will reduce nipping overtime. When you are interacting with the bird, stay calm. You must approach them gently and even keep your talking voice low when interacting with the bird.

Understand the personality of your bird. While humans love to cuddle and play, some birds may not really be fond of it. If your rainbow lorikeet has shown you signs that he needs his space, respect that and find other ways to interact with your bird. That way, he is less stressed and will be calmer.

Teaching your bird not to bite
It is possible to train your rainbow lorikeet not to bite. There are three things that you can do:

- When your bird bites, push the beak down gently or just blow in the bird's face. This is a little uncomfortable for the bird and he will reduce biting when you do this often.

- If the bird is on your hand when he bites, just shake your hand. You can run if the bird is on your shoulder. This is a great way to make the bird lose focus and release the grip on your finger. In addition to that,

Chapter 4: Caring for your Rainbow Lorikeet

being on a shaky perch is very uncomfortable for birds and they will immediately learn that biting is not a good thing.

- Putting the bird on the floor will make them less aggressive, as this is a new territory that makes them feel vulnerable.

When your bird bites, you will reinforce the behavior by pulling away or shouting. It is a better idea to actually push your hand or finger towards the bird to make them release the grip. Pulling away is the reaction that your bird is hoping for and when you do the opposite you actually surprise them.

Preventing screaming or separation anxiety
Separation anxiety in rainbow lorikeets can be heartbreaking and frustrating at the same time. If your bird is crying out in distress every time you leave the room, he may have developed separation anxiety. It is actually very stressful for a bird to be away from the human that he has bonded with. When you feel sorry for your bird, you actually feed into this behavior that can be stressful for you, the bird and the people around you.

The first thing that you need to do is to stop trying to calm your bird down. Even a reprimand such as "no" or "stop" is reinforcement for the bird. He thinks of it as a response to the call. You must get out of his sight and reward him when he is quiet. Even if he is able to stop screeching for a few minutes, return and reward the bird.

Distracting your bird will also help prevent separation anxiety. When your bird is engaged in something else, he will completely forget that you even left the room.

Just before you are about to leave, place a foraging toy in the cage. You can even scrunch up a paper with treats and leave it in the cage. Leaving a window open is also a good idea, as it will give your bird something to watch or will offer ample distraction when you are away. It will also teach the bird that being alone and independent is quite a good thing actually.

Make the ritual of leaving really calm. Avoid any interaction with your bird for at least half an hour before you leave initially. You will be able to reduce this time as your bird gets more used to being on his own. Saying bye to your bird or waving at him will make him anxious. The best thing to do is to leave calmly when your bird is settled in.

Give your bird good physical exercise with toys. You also have to provide your bird with ample mental stimulation. When your bird's energy is all drained out, he is less likely to screech for long periods of time. They will want to rest and will do so even if you are away.

If you are unable to work on the behavior issues on your own, you may consult your vet or can look for a bird trainer who will be able to provide you with tips. Dealing with behavioral issues is the key to building a good relationship with your bird. Remember that they will be with you for close to four decades and you will not be able to put up with bad behavior for too long.

Chewing
While chewing is a natural behavior for birds, it can become a problem when chewing is directed at your valuable belongings. In the wild, a parrot will chew on branches and twigs to make his nest or home "customized".

Chewing is also very important for the bird to maintain his beak and keep it sharp. However, when it is not supervised and directed correctly, chewing can even become hazardous. For instance, a bird can chew on electric wires and get electrocuted or even start an electrical fire.

It is necessary for you to "parrot proof" your home to make it safe for the bird and also to keep your valuables out of the way. You can bring your bird several toys that they are allowed to chew on. This includes cuttlebones, branches, hard toys and lots more. Keep rotating these toys over the weeks to ensure that your bird remains interested in them.

Also make sure that your bird is always supervised when he is out of the cage. There is always a chance of accidents when you fail to do so.

5. Traveling with rainbow lorikeets
Travelling with your bird can be a lot of fun. It is also a great way to bond with your bird. In some cases, it may become a necessity, as you may have to change homes or travel for a long period of time.

Chapter 4: Caring for your Rainbow Lorikeet

Travelling is stressful for the bird. However, there are a few things that you can do to make this less stressful.

For birds, the biggest cause for stress is change. The more familiarity you try to bring when you are training your bird, the happier he will be. Now, the degree or the intensity of anxiety varies from one bird to another.

Some birds may just become comfortable on day one and for others it can mean several health issues and extreme anxiety. Here is a step-by-step process to help you make this easier for your bird:

- Get the bird a travel carrier. The first step is to get the bird used to this carrier. Make it a fun place by providing treats and toys every time the bird gets into this carrier without any sign of anxiety or fear. The best thing to do would be to open the door of the carrier and allow the bird to enter it on his own.

- Once the bird is entering the travel carrier, you can practice leaving him in there for a couple of hours. They are less likely to stress out while the carrier is still in the house, which has several familiar smells and sounds. You may even consider keeping the bird in the cage a few days before you actually have to take a long drive in the car.

- The next step is to introduce the bird to the car. Take the carrier and place it in the car for a few minutes and bring the bird back home. If the bird is stressed and shows signs by fluttering or even breathing with the beak open, take him back and try again until he is relaxing in the carrier when it is taken into the car.

- Then, you can drive around the block with the bird carrier in the backseat. A short five minute drive will help the bird get used to the movement. You do not have to make any elaborate preparations during this drive except lining the floor of the cage with a few extra layers of substrate.

- Now, the calmer you are, the calmer your bird is going to be. Stay relaxed when you are driving the bird. Avoid conversations, music and making too many noises when you are driving the bird around.

Chapter 4: Caring for your Rainbow Lorikeet

- You may gradually increase the time that the bird spends in the moving car. For any trip that is longer than 15 minutes, make sure that you make enough water available. Using a bird water bottle is advisable when you are driving to avoid any spillage and dampness. The cage must be kept lined with enough substrate.

- Watch for signs of stress. The bird will keep the beak open, will retreat to a corner of the cage or will remain on the floor. The idea of being off balance is very stressful to the bird. With a moving car, this is one of the biggest issues. If the bird is getting very anxious, simply drive back home and put the bird in a quiet room. Do not try to verbally comfort your bird, as it only causes more stress.

- When the bird is in the car, make sure that the windows are rolled up to prevent any drafts. You must keep the air conditioner on at room temperature. Since the bird is already under stress, temperature changes due to drafts or the air conditioner will only put the bird at risk.

- If you are going to be travelling with several bags, you might want to include them in the practice drives. The suitcases can be oddly shaped, too large or brightly colored. If the bird is caught off guard on the day of the trip, your training efforts will just not pay off.

- If the travel period is longer than 20 minutes, take breaks to give your bird some food and water. While food is actually needed only twice a day, water is a must at regular intervals. Avoid treats and overfeeding when your bird is traveling, as it will make them sick.

- Birds are unable to poop when they do not have a steady perch. This is another reason why you must stop your car at regular intervals.

- Never take the carrier out of the car. There is always the slightest chance of the door being improperly shut and the bird getting away. It is a risk that you must never take when you are outdoors. It can become really challenging to find your rainbow lorikeet, even though

Chapter 4: Caring for your Rainbow Lorikeet

they are poor fliers. Even when the wings of the bird are clipped, the smallest breeze can give them the lift that they need to get away.

- You can even provide a sleeping tent or throw a blanket over half the carrier. That will give your bird a good place to retreat to incase he feels threatened or scared. They will also rest better when they have a cozy corner to cuddle up in.

- Watch out for signs of overheating and chilling. We will discuss this in the following chapters. Sometimes, the air conditioner may be too cold or the exhaust fumes can lead to overheating in the bird. Provide the necessary first aid as mentioned in the following chapter.

Every time you travel by car with your bird, keep the car quiet. Sounding the horn, laughing, signing or talking loudly will be a stressor to the bird until he gets used to the car.

After the drive, take the bird home and let him relax in a quiet area of the house. Avoid forcing him to play, approaching him or talking to him for an hour or two. That is usually how long he will take to get over the ride and settle into his previous environment. Then he is fully stress free.

Travelling by air
There are times when you have to move or have to travel to a new city or country because of a job or some other commitment. Now, the challenging part is to take your pet bird with you. Especially since rainbow lorikeets are considered exotic birds and are also listed under those that are endangered, you have to take care of several legal procedures as well.

If you are methodical and try to gather as much information as possible, it may not be so hard to manage traveling overseas with your bird. Here are the steps you will follow:

- Visit your vet. He or she is the best person to give you the information that you need about traveling with rainbow lorikeets. You can visit the official website of the Convention on International Trade in Endangered Species or CITES to understand what permits you need.

Chapter 4: Caring for your Rainbow Lorikeet

You will need to contact the US Fish and Wildlife Department or their contemporaries in your country. In some countries this process will take close to seven months, so plan in advance.

- You will require a health certificate for your bird to travel with most airlines. The health certificate must be prepared as per the guidelines of the authorities of the country that you plan to travel to.

- Make a list of all the travel requirements of the major airlines. You must be sure that a certain airline that you choose allows birds to travel with them. You have to reserve a spot for your bird well in advance. This is because the number of pets allowed on board is limited in all airlines. Be sure to take a look at the pet policies of the airline that you choose in complete detail to avoid any last minute surprises or complications with respect to your bird's trip.

- You have to make sure that your bird has the right travel carrier. With airlines you have different requirements for in cabin use and cargo use. You must read about the dimensions and the weight of the carrier.

Make sure that the carrier is spacious enough for the bird. The bird must be able to stretch and flap his wings. There must be ample space to include the food and water bowls, a toy and a perch for the bird. To ease your bird's trip, make sure that he has ample space to perch. There are several airline-approved bird carriers that you can purchase online.

It is best that you avoid any type of travel, by air or by road, during the summer months. In case you have to travel without your bird, make sure that you have reliable foster care. You can even hire a good pet sitter from a reputable agency. Make sure you conduct a lengthy interview in order to be sure of their experience with birds of this kind. Leave the bird's health records and the details of his vet with anyone who is taking care of your bird and make sure that you authorize at least one person to take health decisions for your bird when needed.

Chapter 4: Caring for your Rainbow Lorikeet

- Just like the transport carrier of your car, you need to make sure that the bird gets familiar with the airline carrier as well. You can ease the transition by letting him spend a few hours in the carrier every day before you actually let him spend several hours in it.

The airline that you choose must be based on recommendations. Make sure that you ask around with other rainbow lorikeet or parrot owners to find one that is reliable and one that will handle the birds with care and even feed them and provide water in the case of a long flight.

Chapter 6: Rainbow Lorikeet Breeding

Rainbow lorikeets are prolific breeders. In one season, these birds are capable of having three or more clutches. These birds can even breed well in captivity. The breeding season usually begins in spring. Birds become sexually mature at about 1-2 years of age.

If you want to prevent breeding between a pair of lorikeets, all you need to do is ensure that they do not get the necessary breeding conditions.

1. Finding the right mate

Rainbow lorikeets are monogamous. This means that they will pick a mate for life. That is why it is very important for you to find the perfect match for your rainbow lorikeet.

If you have a single rainbow lorikeet at home, introducing a mate can be tricky. When they are hormonal, females especially, tend to be territorial and aggressive. She is the one that sets the tone of the courting period. If the birds are left unsupervised, the female can cause severe injuries and can potentially kill the male bird.

You will know that a female rainbow lorikeet is ready to mate when you see her spending a lot of time in the nesting box. You must never introduce a male companion immediately. Start by placing the cage of the male bird near the female's cage and allow them to get used to one another.

When the female is adjusted to the presence of her potential mate, she will show signs of being interested in him. To begin with, she will be seen clinging on to the cage bar on the side that is close to the cage of the male bird.

The male will respond by pinning his eyes and the female will keep her head tilted backwards. Even when they are in this stage, it is advisable to keep them apart. You can do this for about one more week until you are certain that the female is interested in the male bird.

Once she shows genuine interest, you can place the birds together. It is best to put them in a different cage altogether. If not, you must put the female bird in the cage of the male and not vice versa. This will prevent excessive territorial behavior from the female. Nevertheless, you can expect the female to chase the male bird around the cage. That is when you need to be extra attentive. If you notice any signs of aggression, it means that you will have to separate them and try again or will have to look for a new mate altogether.

During the introduction, clipping the wings of the female bird is a good idea while keeping the wings of the male intact. That way, the female will have enough flight to reach up to the nesting box. As for the male bird, he will be able to escape any sudden attack.

If you want to pair two birds in particular but are finding it hard to get them to be compatible, you can try by changing the location of the cage or putting them in a new cage. When they are introduced in a completely unfamiliar environment, they tend to bond with one another and will also become less aggressive.

Make sure that new interactions are supervised for a few weeks to let the birds become comfortable with one another.

The other option is to house a pair together all year round. This is a better option, as the aggressive behavior is curbed. Since the female has bonded with the male over the year, the chances of her trying to attack him will be highly reduced.

They become more affectionate towards one another and will do everything together throughout the year. Then when the breeding season arrives, they will show more interest in one another.

After this, you can be sure that they will mate and lay their first clutch. Keeping a pair together for a year is a lot more beneficial. You will be able to maintain proper records. You will also be able to predict the types of mutations that may occur with the birds you pair.

2. Preparing the nesting box

The cage needs to be prepared for lorikeets to be able to breed properly. It is a good idea to give them a separate cage that is enough to accommodate one pair. A smaller cage than the regular one can be used.

The good thing about these birds is that they do not require a fancy nesting box. Any size and shape is good enough for them as long as the pair can fit in comfortably. You can use an elongated cardboard box that measures about 10 inches in depth and height and about 24 inches in length. Using boxes that have an internal shelf can help you with your bird. As these birds tend to push out most of the bedding when they are about to lay eggs, you will have to provide them with new bedding every time. With an internal shelf-type nesting box, the bedding will collect in the bottom and you can just replace it as long as it is clean.

It is best that you provide your bird with lot of natural light. If that is not possible, then you can use a fluorescent light. Full spectrum lights can be placed near the cage to give the bird about 13 hours of daylight. If the light is provided for longer, the birds will breed all year long.

Position the breeding cage against the wall in a quiet area. This will give your bird a sense of security. When they are against the wall, they know that they will not have any threat from that side.

3. Hatching and Incubating

Once the pair settles into the nesting box, you can expect the first clutch to be laid anytime.

The eggs of the rainbow lorikeet are the size of a quarter and are laid every alternate day until the clutch is complete. The number of eggs in a clutch can vary from 3 to 6 eggs. The eggs are white in color.

One interesting thing about all parrots is that the eggs are white in color so that the parent birds can locate them easily in the wild. You see, in their natural habitat, parrots choose dark areas like the cavities of trees to nest. The white eggs are easily visible.

On average, a pair of rainbow lorikeets will produce two clutches every year. It is also possible for them to lay up to three clutches. For the bird to lay three clutches, you will have to remove the eggs from the nest as soon as the clutch is complete.

If you do practice this, make sure that your birds get additional calcium supplements in the form of leafy vegetables or mineral blocks to help them get enough nutrition.

It is best to allow the mother to incubate the eggs. In case you find that she is unable to do so because of behavioral or health issues, you can place your parrot eggs in an artificial incubator.

You will be able to find incubators at pet stores and also online. The settings can be adjusted as per the species of bird. Make sure that you turn the eggs as suggested by the manufacturer.

Usually, incubating rainbow lorikeet eggs takes about 25 days. When the female is incubating her eggs, she will spend most of her time sitting on the eggs. She will only leave the nest to eat and to stretch her wings out every once in a while.

The mother bird will also turn the eggs to ensure that the development of the embryo is even. This also prevents issues like the embryo sticking to one side of the shell.

Just about 2 days before the eggs hatch, the chick will begin to poke a hole from inside. With this hole, the bird gets access to more oxygen, starting the hatching process.

If the weather conditions in the state or city that you live in tend to be dry, having a spray bottle with clean water handy is a good idea. Spray some water inside the nesting box to make the hatching process more comfortable for the baby bird.

The hatching process begins after a hatching ring has been made around the egg. This should take about 15 minutes. After this ring has been made, the chick will maneuver himself out of the egg.

He will break the egg into two sections using his legs. Once the chick has pushed himself out of the egg, the mother bird will remove the eggshells. In case she fails to do so, you can do it yourself to prevent the shell from covering other eggs and leading to complications when they begin to hatch.

4. Nutrition for brooding birds

You need to give your bird a good diet to stay healthy during the breeding season. The female may require calcium supplements to ensure that the eggshells are intact. You will give the bird the regular diet to prevent any stress. You can just add vitamin and mineral supplements to their diet and even give them a cuttlebone to chew on.

If your bird is already on a pellet diet with fresh produce, you only have to worry about giving them the pellets recommended for the breeding period. No added supplementation is necessary with pellets, as they are already fortified. You can place a cuttlebone just in case and the bird will chew on it if she needs the calcium.

5. Caring for the chicks

Hand-raised chicks are certainly tamer, but if you do not really need a very tame chick, co-parenting with your rainbow lorikeet is a good idea. You can provide one meal while the parents provide the others. You can work your way up by increasing the number of feeds you give the baby birds.

You may have to hand-raise the baby entirely if the eggs have been hatched in an incubator or if the mother abandons the nest. This will require some commitment and a lot of patience.

You will have to feed the baby birds every two hours, even at night. So, you need to be entirely sure that you can continue to do so before you take on this responsibility.

In case you are unable to hand-feed the bird or if you think that it is too much work, you can contact your avian vet. There are also several breeders who will be able to foster the chicks.

Ideally, the mother bird should provide for her babies. This will allow the mother to transfer certain nutrients into the baby's body that will help them develop a strong immune system.

What you need to know about hand feeding
- It is a tedious task. Newborn chicks are difficult to handle, as they will move around a lot and will get away from you in a jiffy.

- The delicate frame of the bird's body can also be very intimidating to handle.

- Make sure your hands are properly disinfected before you can handle the baby bird.

- If the eggs have been hatched in an incubator, do not feed the bird for up to 6 hours after hatching. If you feed the baby too early, it could be fatal.

- If you are co-parenting the bird, you must first place it in a brooder with an internal temperature of 95 degree Fahrenheit. When the baby is warmed up, you can feed him. If you feel like he is panting or showing discomfort, reduce the temperature.

- When the baby is warm enough, you can feed him. In case the crop is already full with the food provided by the parent birds, wait for it to empty. If food is present in the crop, a milky fluid is seen in the area.

- A syringe or an eyedropper is ideal to feed the baby birds.

Hand feeding tips for one day old rainbow lorikeet chicks
- The food must be warm and should be about 105-108 degrees Fahrenheit in temperature.

- If it is the first feed of the bird, using only an electrolyte solution is recommended.

- The feeding utensils should be cleaned thoroughly.

- The baby should be kept warm at all times. If the body becomes too cool, the digestion process is hampered.

- The bedding in the brooder should be changed every time you feed your baby bird.

- If there is any abnormality, contact your avian vet immediately.

- If your chick is refusing to eat, do not force him.

- The crop should never be over filled, as it can lead to issues like sour crop.

- A couple of drops should be good enough during the bird's first few feeds.

- The bird should be fed every two hours or just before the crop is fully empty.

The first feed

The bird must be handled very gently to make sure that you do not startle or injure the baby bird. Here are a few important guidelines to make the first feeding session less stressful.

- It is recommended that you use some electrolyte solution such as pedialyte that is not flavored.

- The purpose of the electrolyte solution is to make sure that the digestive abilities of the bird are fine.

- When he has emptied the crop, he is ready for the commercially prepared bird formula.

- To give the bird electrolytes, place a small drop on the left side of the bird's mouth. On most cases, the baby will lap it up immediately.

- In case the baby does not show any interest in the food, you have the option of letting him rest for some time and then trying again.

- Some baby chicks will have to practice before they are able to understand how to take in handfed food.

- If after several attempts your baby bird is not taking any food in, it is possible that the food is not warm enough.

- Dipping the syringe or ink dropper in a glass of warm water before feeding the bird is the best way to keep it warm enough.

Why hand feeding is recommended for rainbow lorikeets

- Rainbow lorikeets are known for abandoning their clutches

- The baby birds are tamer when hand-tamed

- Sometimes, the parents will pluck at the feathers of the babies

- The number of clutches per season increases.

6. Weaning

You can wean a baby bird when he is about 4 weeks old. Weaning means to make the bird capable of eating his food without any assistance.

This will take some understanding and training for your baby bird, so you need to be as patient as possible. Begin by leaving cubes of fresh fruits or some pureed fruit on the floor of the cage and let the bird inspect it. Since rainbow lorikeets are curious by nature, they will peck at it and try to understand the new food.

They may just leave the food alone and walk away or may try to take a piece off. Let the bird explore and after one hour of providing fresh fruits and vegetables, the cage should be cleaned out to prevent the chances of spoiling foods lying around the cage.

As the bird gets familiar with the new food, he will eat bits of it. Take a note of the types of fruits and vegetables that your bird seems to like and include them in the diet.

Soon, you will see that the bird will begin to lose interest in the formula, as he will be full with the food that he has eaten by himself. You can even try to leave pellets and seeds in the water bowl. As the quantity of eating foods on their own increases, the need for assistance will decrease. That way you will have a bird that has been weaned correctly.

Chapter 7: Rainbow Lorikeet Healthcare

Since rainbow lorikeets belong to the family of true parrots, all the common diseases that affect parrots also affect these birds. The first step is to be able to identify any chance of illness in the bird. Then you can take necessary measures to prevent and treat any illness.

1. Identifying illnesses in rainbow lorikeets

The first step towards knowing if your bird needs any medical attention is to be able to identify if he is healthy or not. There are some signs that you will see when the bird's health is deteriorating. Keep an eye out for the slightest change in the bird's normal behavior. If the symptoms are severe, it also means that the infection or health issue is severe.

The earlier you catch the condition, the higher are the chances of your bird getting medical attention before the issue is permanent or irreversible. These are the signs you must watch out for:

- The beak develops spots or abnormalities. If the beak is dry and is peeling or has any discharge, it is an indication of health issues.

- The bird is bleeding.

- Breathing is very difficult and strained.

- The bird lets out sharp coughs.

- Drooling is a common sign of yeast infection.

- The eyes of the bird seem to be red, swollen or runny.

- The skin seems to be itchy or sore. The bird may have bald patches or abnormal falling of feathers even when it is not the molting season.

- The bird is plucking out his own feathers.

- The position of the head is abnormal. This may manifest in the form of circling of the head or twisting that seems unusual. The head may even twitch or shake in some cases.

- The head has wet feathers and seem soiled. This is a sign that the bird has been vomiting, especially if the wetness is restricted to the head.

- The joints of the bird seem to be swollen and the bird is less mobile or is hesitating to stand up.

- The legs seem weak or may even be paralyzed.

- The droppings have more urine or have an abnormal color or consistency.

- The bird experiences seizures from time to time.

- The vent or the cloaca of the bird is swollen or has some soreness around it.

- The crop or the abdomen of the bird is extremely swollen.

- There are lumps or tumors on the body.

- The bird seems to have lost his voice or the voice of the bird shows sudden changes.

- The wings are drooping.

- The bird shows sudden fluctuations in his weight.

- Vomiting is a common sign of illness. Regurgitation is a common behavior in parrots. When the bird regurgitates, the undigested food is thrown out. If there are not food particles in the expulsion, it might indicate vomiting.

- The bird is refusing to leave the floor of the cage.

- The bird seems to be lethargic and uninterested in the toys.

- Food consumption reduces drastically or increases significantly.

- The bird may consume excess water or may not drink water at all.

With these signs, you can be sure that your bird needs medical attention. When neglected, the issue will escalate, often leading to sudden death in the bird. The more you interact with your birds, the more likely you are to observe even the smallest drift from normalcy.

2. Nutritional Deficiencies

Rainbow lorikeets mostly suffer from nutritional deficiencies. Some of them are more common that others. Here are some of the most important nutritional deficiencies in rainbow lorikeets:

Obesity

This condition is prevalent in many pet parrots. They are given a diet of high fat nuts, seeds and even table scraps. In some cases, overfeeding and not providing the bird with enough exercise will lead to obesity.

When a bird is about 20% over the ideal weight, it is said to be obese. The weight of the bird's body will lead to lameness, while he may experience respiratory issues if the concentration of the weight is in the abdominal area.

If your bird is diagnosed with obesity, it is a good idea to change the diet to a pelleted one with adequate portion control. Encourage your bird to exercise by keeping several food bowls around the cage to encourage him to walk around. Climbing and balancing toys also improves the physical activity of your bird.

Vitamin A deficiency
Vitamin A is one of the most important nutrients in a bird's diet, as it affects the immune system. Seed diets that contain even 50% seed and 50% pellet lead to vitamin a deficiency or hypovitaminosis A.

The symptoms of vitamin A deficiency include:

- Sneezing
- Nasal discharge
- Periorbital swelling
- Conjunctivitis
- Dyspnea
- Excessive urination
- Excessive water consumption
- Blunt or absent papilla
- Anorexia
- Development of white plaques in the sinuses and eyes.

The treatment process involves dealing with the secondary infections if any and supplementing the bird's diet with Vitamin A. You can add natural sources like spirolina to the food of the bird to get better results.

Iodine deficiency
Although this condition is not very prevalent with the fortified pet foods, you need to be aware that a deficiency of iodine can lead to goiter or thyroid hyperplasia.

The most common symptoms are:

- Wheezing
- Clicking
- Respiratory stridor.

You can use Lugol's iodine until the signs of iodine deficiency have subsided or been removed completely.

Calcium, Vitamin D3, Phosphorous deficiency
Most seed-based diets will lead to a deficiency in calcium, amino acids and phosphorous. These seeds are also quite high in their fat content.

Metabolic bone disease
If the bird has an imbalanced calcium to phosphorous ration, there are chances that he will develop hyperthyroidism. This is most common in younger and old birds.

Along with a lack of calcium, most birds have to cope with a deficiency in Vitamin D3, as they are housed indoors without adequate access to sunlight.

In the case of younger birds, a lack of calcium in the diet will result in deformation and curvature in the longer bones as well as the vertebrae.

The common signs of metabolic bone disease are:
- Ataxia
- Seizures
- Deformation
- Repeated fractures
- Thin shelled eggs
- Decreased egg production and hatchability
- Death of the embryo
- Egg binding.

The plasma calcium levels are studied to diagnose a possible deficiency in calcium levels. Supportive care along with necessary vitamin D and calcium supplementation is the best option. It also a good idea to provide your birds with a full spectrum light if they do not have enough access to natural sunlight. In the case of recurring fractures, bandaging and cage rest is necessary with adequate doses of painkillers.

If you can provide your bird with an outdoor cage, it will allow them to get natural light in abundance. If your bird's wings have been clipped, they can be taken outdoors provided you keep a close eye on them.

Vitamin D toxicosis
While excessive oral calcium does not cause any health issues in birds, if you give them too much oral vitamin D3, there could be an accumulation of calcium in the tissues of the body including the kidneys. Make sure that you provide supplements only after consulting the vet.

Iron storage disease
The condition of having excessive accumulation of iron in the liver is called iron storage disease. It is also called hemachromatosis. As the level of iron increases, the lysozomes in the liver get damaged and release ions that lead to damage by oxidization in the membranes of the organs. It also leads to an improper metabolism of proteins

Iron storage disease is not very common in pet birds but they are constantly at risk if proper diet is not provided. If the intake of iron is too high, it leads to this condition. There are other factors like genetic predisposition and stress that can cause this condition. Even an increased vitamin C intake will lead to storage of iron in the body.

The most commonly affected organs are the heart, liver and spleen. The signs of iron storage disease include:

- Weight loss
- Depression
- Distended abdomen
- Dyspnea
- Circulatory failure.

The condition can be diagnosed with a biopsy of the liver. Treatment normally includes modification of the diet and removal of iron from the body. You must provide the bird with a lot of fiber to prevent accumulation of iron in the liver.

Other nutritional concerns
- A bird may develop sensitivity to certain preservatives and dyes present in pellets.

- They may experience a failure in the right side of the heart if the diet consists mainly of seeds.

- Improperly stored food will lead to cirrhosis.

- Your bird may not be eating everything that you provide even if you are making the effort of giving them a balanced meal. This must be dealt with by providing adequate supplements.

- If you are adding supplements, make sure that the bird is observed properly. Usually, these supplements are not palatable and the bird may stop consuming water, leading to dehydration.

- Never give your bird any foods that contain caffeine, alcohol, salt, refined sugar or dairy products.

In the wild, lorikeets spend most of their time foraging. In the case of pet birds, they have access to one food bowl that gives them the entire caloric intake. However, with less energy spent, they will develop nutritional issues. Make sure that your bird has a healthy lifestyle.

It is a must to provide your bird with toys and adequate mental stimulation. A large enough cage is the first step to helping your bird burn some energy if it has enough toys and stimulators.

3. Common Lorikeet Health Issues
Some diseases that commonly affect rainbow lorikeets are as follows:

Polyoma
This disease normally affects birds that are younger, most often just when they are born. Adults will develop immunity to this disease over time.

The disease is caused by a virus called the Polyoma Virus.

Symptoms:
There are very few external symptoms for this condition.

- The bird will die suddenly within 48 hours of contracting the disease, often with no symptoms at all.

Treatment:
- Make sure that the birds are vaccinated as soon as they are born.

- Preventive care is the best way to make sure that your bird is safe.

- Adopt proper quarantine practices.

- Make sure that people who have been in contact with other birds wash their hands and feet completely before you allow them to interact with your bird.

- Maintain a hygienic environment for your bird to live in.

Beak and feather syndrome
This condition is also known as Psittacine Beak and Feather Disease and mostly affects cockatoos. However, several cases of rainbow lorikeets developing the condition have been reported. This condition affects older birds in most cases.

Symptoms:
- The feathers seem to be gnarled and swollen.

- New feathers that develop after molting will look abnormal.

- Beak will look dull and dusty, as it is covered with feather dust.

- The development of the beak is abnormal.

- In extreme cases, it can also lead to paralysis in the bird.

Treatment:
- There is no remedy for PBFD and the bird will either die or will become a carrier.

- It is best to isolate any bird that is infected.

- Sometimes, when the condition is very severe, euthanizing is the only option.

- Since the condition is usually spread by feces and feather dander, proper hygiene can help control the condition.

Proventricular Dilation Disease
Also known as Macaw Wasting Disease, this condition is common in all parrot breeds. It is highly contagious but stays dormant for several years. Therefore, it is a very difficult disease to diagnose.

Symptoms:
Seizures
- Heart attacks
- Tremors
- Paralysis
- Lack of coordination.

Treatment:
- There is no medication that is known to treat this condition yet.

- Make sure that you include digestible supplements in the diet of your bird after consulting an avian vet.

- Changing the diet of the bird is also useful in prolonging his life.

Papilloma
This condition will most often affect the vent area of the bird and in some cases, the throat and the mouth. While the disease in itself is not fatal, the papilloma can choke the bird when it develops in the throat and mouth.

Symptoms:
- Wart-like growth in the vent area or in the throat and mouth.

- Changed behavior in the bird.

- Labored breathing due to blocked respiratory tract.

Treatment:
- Laser surgery to remove the growth.

- Surgical removal of this unwanted growth.

Psittacosis

This condition is commonly known as parrot fever and is a disease that can affect a bird at any age. It is caused by highly potent bacteria that belong to the same strain that causes chlamydosis in pet birds.

Symptoms:
- Nasal discharge
- Sneezing
- Sinusitis
- Conjunctivitis
- Pneumonia
- Lime green colored droppings
- Seizures
- Tremors
- Paralysis
- Death.

Treatment:
- Tetracycline drugs are administered.

- The most recommended medicine today is doxycycline.

- The medication is normally administered through the drinking water, but if the bird does not drink medicated water, they can be injected too.

- The cage and aviary must be cleaned and disinfected after treatment.

- Preventive measures are a must, as this can lead to Chlamydia in people.

E-coli infection
E-coli bacteria are part of the flora of the body of parrots. This means that the microorganism lives in the digestive tract of your rainbow lorikeet and actually benefits the bodily functions.

However, disease and untimely death is possible when the bacteria enter the reproductive system, the respiratory system or the bloodstream of the bird.

Symptoms:
- Ruffled feathers
- Diarrhea
- Listlessness
- Weakness
- Shivering
- Vent picking.

Treatment:
- Culturing the bacteria and testing them for antibiotic susceptibility is the first step.

- It benefits to understand if the bacteria is causing a certain disease of if your bird is experiencing some form of secondary infection.

- Coliform infections are common in the respiratory system and that is when it could be fatal.

- Keeping the bird's environment clean goes a long way in preventing this condition.

- Keep the inside and the outside of the cage as clean as possible.

Gout

Gout is the result of calcification in the kidneys. Young birds that do not receive a proper balance of calcium in the diet can be susceptible. This is a disease which is primarily diet related.

The formula that you give the baby bird should be suitable to its metabolism to prevent gout.

Symptoms:
- The initial symptoms are very mild.
- Regurgitation of the food and dehydration occurs in the initial stages.
- The baby bird looks smaller than usual.
- High concentration of urates are revealed with blood tests.
- The skin on the chest looks wrinkled.
- The bird is unable to retain anything, including fluids in the crop.
- When the symptoms become obvious, your bird is possibly close to the end of its life.

Treatment:
- Keep the baby bird well hydrated.

- Probenecid or Colochicine is administered to keep the heart safe.

- Urates can be removed from the bloodstream with Allopurinal.

Aspergillosis

This airborne disease affects the lungs of the bird. It is caused by a fungal infection due to improper cage sanitation. If the food is damp and spoilt, it will become a harboring site for the fungi. In addition to that, cage grates and food or water bowls with fecal deposits will lead to fungal infections. Low humidity and dust in the environment also lead to this infection.

Symptoms:
- Lack of appetite
- Reduced or excessive consumption of water

- Change in the voice
- Depression
- Excessive urination
- Lethargy
- Change in the behavior
- Paralysis
- Ataxia or loss of muscle control.

Treatment:
- Inrtacocozole and Fluconozole are administered.

- Keeping the environment of the bird is a preventive measure.

- Make sure that you only give your bird clean and fresh food and water.

Salmonellosis

This is a very serious bacterial infection in birds. It can also be passed on to humans. With parrots, the mortality rate is very high and it also leads to many carriers if even one bird in your flock is infected. In the acute stage, the condition is normally treated with antibiotics. However, for the most part, the birds will not show any symptoms.

Treatment:
- The fecal culture of newborn birds should be screened. This helps reveal if a bird is shedding.

- Infected birds should never be bred.

- If you want to breed the bird, make sure that it is isolated with its partner and that all the eggs are artificially incubated.

Sinusitis

The exact cause of the condition remains unknown. It is one disease that is quite complex and can be highly contagious.

Symptoms:

- Respiratory problems such as breathlessness
- Labored breathing.

Remedy:
- If the causal factor is a secondary infection, it is a little more complex to treat.

- Providing vitamin A supplement has proved useful in most cases.

Proteus and pseudomonas infection
This infection can affect the eyes, the digestive system and the upper and lower respiratory system among other organs. This condition is caused when the bird consumes spoilt food. Poor hygiene also leads to infections.

Symptoms:
Lack of appetite
- Diarrhea
- Urinary problems
- Breathing difficulties
- Nasal discharges
- Eye infections
- Tremors
- Seizures.

Treatment:
- Antibiotic susceptibility tests on the culture is needed to develop a long term treatment process.

- Pseudomonas are resistant to most antibiotics.

Molting
This is a very stressful condition for your bird. This is when the old feathers are shed and new feathers grow in their place.

Symptoms:
- Less active
- Very irritable
- A keratin cuticle that appears like a waxy layer is removed as the bird preens itself
- After the new feathers have grown, the bird spends a lot of time preening and almost appears like he is scratching himself all the time.
- There are also chances that you will notice pieces of this cuticle on the body of the bird. It is very easy to mistake this for feather dander.

Treatment:
- The bird should not have any stressors in his environment.

- A balanced diet with vitamin supplements is necessary.

- You can mist the body of the bird regularly to make the irritation lesser.

- It also helps to give the birdbaths frequently.

- You can also make sure that your bird gets enough rest.

- If, in the process of preening, the bird is damaging his own feathers, you must contact your vet immediately. This could indicate behavioral issues like feather plucking.

The most vital thing with rainbow lorikeet health is to maintain a clean environment and to provide good food. There must not be any room for the pathogens to thrive if you want to make sure that your bird is safe at all times. Regular vet checkups will help detect any disease at an early stage and thus provide better options to treat the condition.

4. Feather plucking in lorikeets

Feather plucking is common in birds, as they use the beak to groom and preen themselves often. The only time it becomes a serious issue is when the bird is actually mutilating himself in the process of plucking the feathers out. The more frequent the feather plucking, the more are the chances of the bird injuring himself. Although it is commonly termed as a behavioral problem, there are several reasons why birds begin to pluck their own feathers, such as:

- Malnutrition
- Cysts on the skin
- Parasitic infections
- Stress
- Boredom
- Cancer
- Liver disease
- Allergies to food or dust
- Inflammation of the skin
- Skin infection
- Heavy metal poisoning
- Metabolic problems
- Dryness in the skin
- Low humidity
- Lack of proper sunlight
- Any disturbance in sleep patterns
- Presence of preservatives or dyes in the food.

You may think that a bird resorts to feather plucking only when he is bored or unhappy. However, even if your bird is too exhausted with less rest, he may begin to pluck his feathers out. A bird that has the problem of feather plucking will be rather aggressive and anxious. This may be very different from the normal demeanor of your beloved bird.

Most often, birds will sudden display feather plucking when they are ready to breed and nest. This is also called brood patch plucking. You know that your bird is plucking due to the breeding instinct because the feathers from the abdominal region and the chest area are plucked out. This is actually done by females to be able to transfer heat during the incubation phase. If your bird is not mated, sexual urges make them pluck their feathers, as they are unable to fulfill this need. Now, if your rainbow lorikeet has bonded with only one person in the house, it is possible that the bird thinks of that person as the mate. When the bird's "mate" showers attention on someone else, say another pet or a new baby, feather plucking is observed.

If your bird is housed in a cage that is too small or if the perch is not comfortable, he may begin to pluck his feathers out. This is because he probably feels uncomfortable and unhappy in his space. If your bird is unable to get enough exercise or mental stimulation, he will chew on his own feathers as an attempt to keep himself entertained.

If you have trimmed the wings of your bird incorrectly, he will begin to pluck his feathers as an attempt to make the feathers more even. Rainbow lorikeets are very sensitive creatures. If they see a lot of emotional turmoil in their home such as constant fighting, they tend to develop anxiety. Even the smallest change in the environment such as the flickering of a light can irritate the bird enough to cause feather plucking.

This can be a really frustrating time for you as well, as the bird may develop habits like chewing, biting, over preening, etc. In order to curb this issue you need to be extremely patient with your bird and first get to the root of the problem. Understand why the bird is behaving in this manner. If you are unable to figure that out for yourself, you can also visit the vet for a consultation. There are some measures that you can take to help alleviate this issue:

- Keep your bird mentally stimulated

- If he is plucking for attention, make sure that you do not give in to it. Instead giving him a time out when he starts plucking tells him that plucking does not get your attention.

- Make sure that the food you give your bird is healthy and adequate.

- Get the feathers clipped by a professional.

- Make sure you have regular health checkups for your bird.

- The day and night lighting should be consistent. If your bird is in a room that has a TV, you might want to give him a sleeping tent so that he can get enough rest.

The problem with feather plucking is that it is not easy to fix. Your bird will always have a tendency to pluck once he begins. In addition, the rate of feather plucking and the duration depends on the cause. For example, if it is because of an infection, you can give him medicines and feather plucking will subside eventually. However, if feather plucking occurs after you got married and your bird is jealous of your spouse, it may take a lot of time for him to give this habit up. On your part, you need to be patient. If you feel like you are unable to help your bird, you can look for assistance from your avian vet. Follow all the instructions precisely and it is possible that your bird will recover soon. The best remedy for feather plucking is preventive care and ensuring that your bird is always healthy and happy.

Feather plucking v/s molting
In particular seasons, you may find several feathers on the floor of your bird's cage. You will also notice bald patches on the bird's body. This is not a cause for concern, as the bird has started molting. Usually, lorikeets begin to molt at the age of 4 months.

Feather plucking is the voluntary removal of feathers and consequently mutilating the body. Molting, on the other hand, is a natural and seasonal process that allows your bird to shed old feathers and grow new ones.

A bird that is molting will be irritable and grumpy, as this is a very uncomfortable phase for the bird. You can help by misting the feathers to relieve itching and burning sensations. You may also change the diet of the bird after consulting the vet to make the molting process less painful for the bird.

5. Finding a good avian vet
Rainbow lorikeets are exotic birds that need specialized care. You can consult a regular vet for any emergency, however, it is important for you to look for an avian vet who has experience working with exotic birds like

rainbow lorikeets. A good avian vet will be able to deal with specific health conditions that affect rainbow lorikeets.

Finding a good vet requires you to do some research. Make sure you do this well before your bird comes home.

The first thing that you need to remember is that you need an avian vet who specializes in treating exotic birds. You should be able to find one located close to you after surfing the Internet. One of the most reliable sources of avian vet listings is the official website of the Association of Avian Vets or www.aav.org. They will list vets as per the locality and state.

Being associated with an avian vet who is affiliated with organizations like the AAV means that the vet is able to stay updated with the current trends in treating birds like rainbow lorikeets, as these organizations have regular seminars and conferences that cover these subjects. There are a few things that you can ask your vet to confirm that your bird is in the right hands:

- How often do they treat birds? Ideally, the vet should be seeing at least 3 avian patients a day. If the number is about 3-4 a month, then the vet is not specialized in these birds. You can seek advice from them in an emergency but you will have to scout for someone with more experience in dealing with these birds.

- What are the methods that they use to keep themselves updated? You may not be able to ask them this question directly but you can certainly ask the vet if he or she is part of any avian vet group or you can ask about the last conference that he or she attended. You can even check for magazine or book subscriptions that the vet may recommend. This will tell you that he or she is genuinely working to gather as much information as possible when it comes to treating the bird.

- What are the types of parrots that they generally treat? This question will give you an idea about the variety of birds that the vet has experience with.

- How long does each examination take? Usually every bird will need a good 30 minutes. If the vet is only giving each bird about 10 minutes, then he or she may be overcrowded. While that speaks for the popularity of the vet, it does not really help your bird too much, as sessions may be hurried.

- What are the emergency services provided? Is the clinic itself open for emergencies? In most cases, they will at least have affiliations with 24-hour services that will be able to tend to your bird in emergencies. Some vets are also available on call, which is certainly the ideal situation. However, they may be occupied with other cases at times and it is best if they are able to provide you with alternatives.

Walking around the clinic will also give you a fair idea about whether you are making the right choice or not. There must be basic amenities like a gram scale.

Observe how the vet handles the bird. If they are examining the bird in the cage, it may be an indication of inexperience unless there is any specific reason for keeping the bird inside the cage.

The staff should also be able to handle the bird comfortably. They must at least be able to identify the species of the bird that you have brought in. That is again an indication that there are avian patients who are often treated at the clinic.

You must also check the in-patient facilities. If they are admitting birds in the clinic after major procedures like surgeries, you will have to ensure that adequate quarantining methods are adopted to prevent any secondary infections in the birds that are admitted there.

Lastly, you must make sure that your vet is located at a convenient location. If not, every visit to the vet will end up being a stressful one for the bird. The vet must not be more than 15 minutes away from your home. This is also ideal when you do have an emergency.

In case your bird needs special care, your vet will be able to recommend the right facility. So, as long as the vet is competent to take care of the bird, it is better to look for a decent facility close to you in comparison to a high end one that is located far away.

You should also be able to build a rapport with your vet. The way they handle your questions and whether they are interested in giving you information about the bird will tell you a lot about the personality of the vet. The vet will be an important part of raising your bird, as you may have queries about your bird's health from time to time.

Once you have made the choice, ensure that everyone in your home has access to the contact details of the vet. They must also be provided to others who may care for your bird, including pet sitters.

6. Rainbow lorikeet first aid

If you see that your bird has had an accident, take him to a quiet room and leave him there with some water. Make sure that you do not panic or scream in front of the bird. This makes it worse for him. Let him calm down and then you can talk to him in a calm and comforting voice. Of course, if the injury is serious, you need to take the bird to the vet immediately. Here are some common accidents that your bird may encounter and the necessary measures you have to take:

- Skin wounds: If the bird has cuts or bruises on the skin, wash it gently with 3% hydrogen peroxide. You can use gauze, Q-tips or cotton to clean the area. In case the skin wound is caused by a cat or dog bite, wash the area and rush the bird to a vet. In order to stop bleeding in the skin, you can use a styptic pencil or you can also use cornstarch.

- Bleeding nail or beak: Sometimes, the bird's beak or nail can get entangled in the wires used to hang toys. It could also get caught in the bars of the cage. Then, you need to apply pressure on the injured area directly using a paper towel or cotton gauze. If that is not good enough, you can use a styptic pencil or cornstarch to control the bleeding.

- Broken blood feathers: Bleeding in the broken blood feathers is profuse and can even be fatal if you do not curb bleeding immediately. Use a styptic pencil to clot blood and hold the area down with gauze or clean tissue paper.

- Burns: If your bird suffers from burns due to a hot stove, hot water, steam or even hot utensils, you can relieve the pain by misting the feathers with cold water. If the leg or foot is burnt, just dip it in cold water. Make sure that the water is not too cold. It should be cold water from the tap, not the refrigerator. You can use an antibiotic cream, but make sure that it is not oil or grease based, as the heat is retained by such creams. In the case of acid burns due to cleaning agents or detergents, flood the area with lots of cold water to relieve the pain.

- Heatstroke: The best thing to do would be to put the bird in an air conditioned room. If you do not use air conditioning in your home, you can use cold water to mist the feathers and then turn on a fan. If you are turning a fan on, make sure that the bird is in a cage. Then, give the bird water to drink. In case of extreme heat stroke, it might become necessary to drop water into the bird's mouth directly.

- Broken bones or wings: It is best that you do not handle a bird with broken bones. This may happen by flying into a window, predator attacks, getting caught between a door, etc. In the case of a broken wing, you can hold the wing close to the body and secure it before transferring the bird to a travel cage. You need to remove any perch or toy from the cage if you are transporting a bird with broken bones. Line the floor with a soft towel with no loops.

7. First aid kit for rainbow lorikeets

In order to provide timely care for your bird in case of an emergency, you need to have an emergency kit ready at all times. Here are a few things that you must include in your first aid kit:

- A blood coagulant: This helps prevent any profuse bleeding. A styptic pencil is the best option. If that is not available, you may use cornstarch or even flour.

- Tweezers: The bandages that you use for your bird will be very small in size. Having a pair of tweezers makes it easier for you to handle them.

- Cotton swabs: Any time you need to clean up a wound, cotton swabs will come in very handy. If you do not have any, you can even use Q-tips.

- Gauze: You need gauze to clean and wrap cuts, bruises and even bites. Sometimes, it also helps secure broken wings or bones.

- Bandages: If you want to have bandages in your bird's first aid box, make sure that they are non-adhesive. Specialized bandages are available for birds in most pet stores.

- Syringe: You will need a syringe to wash small wounds or the eyes of the bird.

- Disinfectants: The best option is hydrogen peroxide, as it removes any germs that might cause infections to your bird.

- Towel: An injured bird can get aggressive and irritated, so using a towel to handle him will make things a lot easier for you.

Keeping a first aid kit handy is important. Also make sure that you are checking the contents for cleanliness and hygiene. If you notice that the bandages are dirty or dusty, replace them immediately. If not, your bird may develop secondary infections that are harder to deal with than the actual injury itself.

8. Preventive Care

There is no better way to keep your bird healthy than preventive care. Since most illnesses spread so fast in rainbow lorikeets, it is best that you take all the precautionary steps possible to prevent this sort of infection in the first place. Here are some tips that will help you maintain the health of your little feathered companion:

- Make sure that the diet is wholesome and nutritious.

- Clean the cage and its contents regularly.

- Take your pet to the vet for an annual checkup without fail.

- Any new bird that is introduced to your home must be quarantined without fail.

- The bird must have a lot of clean water to drink.

- Your bird must be mentally stimulated in order to ensure good health.

- Spend enough time with your bird to prevent any behavioral problems.

- You need to make sure that he gets ample sunlight. It is a good idea to take the bird outdoors provided he is harnessed or is protected by a cage.

- Your home must be bird proofed even before you bring the bird home.

- Grooming and cleaning the bird is necessary.

Always keep your vet's number handy and learn as much as you can about your rainbow lorikeet's health. That way, communicating with the vet also becomes easier and you will be able to provide better care for your bird.

Chapter 8: Cost of Having a Rainbow Lorikeet

There are some constant expenses that you need to be prepared for when you bring home a rainbow lorikeet. A break-up of these expenses is as follows:

- Cost of the bird: $600 and upwards or £400 and upwards.
- Cage: $600-1000 or £350-700.
- Food and water bowls: $8-30 or £2-20.
- Four to five toys: $20-100 or £10-75.
- Perch: $6-15 or £3-10.
- Ladder: $8-20 or £3-15.
- Play stand: $30-200 or £15-100.
- Cleaning supplies: $30 or £20.
- Formulated Food (1 packet): £9-20 or £5-10.
- Travel carrier: $25-80 or £10-50.
- Veterinary exam (one)- $50-200 or £25-70.

The total beginning supply costs will vary from $300-1200 or £150-700. This does not include variable costs like the cost of fresh produce.

Conclusion

I hope that you have had fun reading this book and understanding all the nuances of bird care. This book has, hopefully, prepared you for your feathered friend. The purpose of this book is to make sure that you are ready to take on the responsibility of a rainbow lorikeet.

Thank you for choosing this book. The efforts in providing you with genuine and practical information are sincere. Hopefully, that will translate into a good relationship with your beloved bird.

Make sure that you take your role as a bird owner seriously. These exquisite birds are a wonder of nature with their amazing cognitive abilities and their perfect temperament to fit into any home that is willing to make the effort.

In your journey with your bird, try to educate yourself as much as you can about your bird. There is no end to how much you can learn. The more you know, the better you can make your bird's life.

References

Learning more about the pets that you have will help you provide better care. There are several books that are available to you about rainbow lorikeet care.

However, for the most recent and updated information, you can find various sources online. There are several forums where you can connect with rainbow lorikeet owners online. You can also read detailed papers about the habits and behavior of these birds. That way, you can improve the care that you provide to your birds consistently.

Here are some websites that you can refer to:

www.members.optusnet.com.au

http://www.birdsinbackyards.net

http://www.birdlife.org.au

www.reptilepark.com.au

www.agric.wa.gov.au

www.australianwildlife.com.au

www.lafeber.com

www.nativesymbols.info

www.write4fun.net

www.wilderutopia.com

www.burkesbackyard.com.au

www.kcbbs.gen.nz/lori/ar/handrear2.html

www.innersouthvets.com.au

www.nzbirdsonline.org.nz

www.birdsnways.com

www.what-when-how.com/birds/rainbow-lorikeet-birds

www.northernparrots.com

www.thespruce.com

www.forums.avianavenue.com

www.parrotforums.com

www.wetcanvas.com

www.theparrotforum.com

www.aussiefinchforum.net

www.talkparrots.com

www.essentialkids.com.au

www.parrotdebate.com

www.gpforums.com.au

www.preciselyparrots.com

Copyright and Trademarks: This publication is Copyrighted 2017 by Zoodoo Publishing. All products, publications, software and services mentioned and recommended in this publication are protected by trademarks. In such instance, all trademarks & copyright belong to the respective owners. All rights reserved. No part of this book may be reproduced or transferred in any form or by any means, graphic, electronic, or mechanical, including photocopying, recording, taping, or by any information storage retrieval system, without the written permission of the authors. Pictures used in this book are either royalty free pictures bought from stock-photo websites or have the source mentioned underneath the picture.

Disclaimer and Legal Notice: This product is not legal or medical advice and should not be interpreted in that manner. You need to do your own due-diligence to determine if the content of this product is right for you. The author and the affiliates of this product are not liable for any damages or losses associated with the content in this product. While every attempt has been made to verify the information shared in this publication, neither the author nor the affiliates assume any responsibility for errors, omissions or contrary interpretation of the subject matter herein. Any perceived slights to any specific person(s) or organization(s) are purely unintentional. We have no control over the nature, content and availability of the web sites listed in this book. The inclusion of any web site links does not necessarily imply a recommendation or endorse the views expressed within them. Zoodoo Publishing takes no responsibility for, and will not be liable for, the websites being temporarily unavailable or being removed from the Internet. The accuracy and completeness of information provided herein and opinions stated herein are not guaranteed or warranted to produce any particular results, and the advice and strategies, contained herein may not be suitable for every individual. The author shall not be liable for any loss incurred as a consequence of the use and application, directly or indirectly, of any information presented in this work. This publication is designed to provide information in regards to the subject matter covered. The information included in this book has been compiled to give an overview of the subject s and detail some of the symptoms, treatments etc. that are available to people with this condition. It is not intended to give medical advice. For a firm diagnosis of your condition, and for a treatment plan suitable for you, you should consult your doctor or consultant. The writer of this book and the publisher are not responsible for any damages or negative consequences following any of the treatments or methods highlighted in this book. Website links are for informational purposes and should not be seen as a personal endorsement; the same applies to the products detailed in this book. The reader should also be aware that although the web links included were correct at the time of writing, they may become out of date in the future.

www.ingramcontent.com/pod-product-compliance
Lightning Source LLC
Chambersburg PA
CBHW061450040426
42450CB00007B/1296